The
Messenger
of
The Cross

The Messenger of the Cross

WATCHMAN NEE

Translated from the Chinese

Christian Fellowship Publishers, Inc.
New York

ISBN 0-935008-50-0

Available from the Publisher at:

11515 Allecingie Parkway
Richmond, Virginia 23235

PRINTED IN U.S.A.

TRANSLATOR'S PREFACE

In the counsel of God's will, the cross occupies a central place. This is because only through the cross can God's eternal purpose concerning His Son as well as His church be realized. "I determined not to know anything among you, save Jesus Christ, and him crucified," declared the apostle Paul (1 Cor. 2.2). Christ came to us by way of the cross, and only by this same way do we know Him. Unless the cross is accepted by us both objectively in terms of the finished work of Christ at Calvary and subjectively in terms of the dealing of the Holy Spirit in us, we have no message to deliver to the world and we are not fit to be its messengers.

In this present volume, Watchman Nee shows us that at the source of all spiritual things stands the cross. In order that Christ may be all and in all, there is no effective means save the cross. How we therefore need to pray, "Search me, O God, and know my heart: try me and know my thoughts" (Ps. 139.23), so that by God's response to such heartfelt prayer we may have a true knowledge of our selves. Now such response will mean our having to experience the dividing of our spirit and soul, since the root of all sins is the fallen self life of man. Yet, as the author makes clear, with the self thus dealt with, we can then be true messengers of the cross.

May God raise up many such messengers today.

CONTENTS

This volume consists of messages either written or delivered by the author over an extended period of anointed ministry of God's word. Because of the relatedness of their content, they are now being translated and published together in English as a single volume.

1 | The Messenger of the Cross

In recent years many seem to have become tired of hearing the message of the cross; yet we thank and praise God our Father, for He has reserved for His great name's sake quite a few faithful who have not bent their knees to Baal. We feel, however, that all servants of God should know why, though they faithfully proclaim the cross, they have so little result. Why is it that people hear the truthful word of God and yet their lives evidence so little change? We believe this matter should receive our greatest attention. We as workers of the Lord ought to know why the gospel we preach fails to gain people. May we humbly pray, asking the Spirit of God to shed His light upon our hearts that we may see wherein we have failed.

Naturally we must pay attention to the word we preach. (We will not here concern ourselves with those who preach a wrong or "another" gospel, since their faith is already in error.) As regards what we preach, it is that truth which is in perfect accord with the Bible. As to our theme, it is the cross of the Lord Jesus. What we proclaim is none other than the Lord Jesus and Him crucified in order to save sinners from both the penalty and power of sin. We know that our Lord died on the cross as the substitute for sinners so that all who believe in Him will be saved without works. Yet we not only know that Christ was crucified as our substitute; we also know that sinners and their sins were crucified with Him too. We are fully acquainted with the way of salvation. We are familiar with the secret of dying with Christ and drawing by faith the power of His death to deal with self as well as with sin. We understand very clearly all the other teachings related to this matter in the Bible; and we can present them so well that all seem to appreciate them — so well, in fact, that when we preach the cross of Christ, the audience seems to be most attentive and quite moved. Perhaps we are naturally eloquent, and this further increases our ability to move people — and adds greatly, we think, to the effect of our work.

Under such circumstances as these, we naturally expect many unbelievers to receive life and many believers to receive life more abundantly. Nevertheless, the results turn out surprisingly differently. Although the audience appears to be quite moved in the auditorium, we find they merely retain in their memory the words spoken without gaining spiritually what we desire for them. There is no notable change in their lives. They understand the teaching but their daily lives are not affected. They simply store what they hear in their minds, without it having any practical impact in their hearts.

The reason for such a contrary effect seems to lie in the fact that what you and I have is mere eloquence, words or wisdom. Behind our spoken word there is not that power which pricks the heart. Our word and voice may excel, yet the power of changing lives is missing in our word and voice. In other words, though we may draw people to listen to us in the auditorium, the Holy Spirit has not worked together with us. And hence our effort leaves no permanent result. Our word does not leave any indelible impression upon people's lives. Out of our mouths words may flow, but out of our spirit no *life* has been released to nourish and quicken the spiritually parched audience.

Lately the word of God has especially called my attention against this kind of preaching. We are not to strive to be orators acclaimed by the people (for is not our Lord the life-giver?); we instead ought to be mere channels through which His life will flow into human hearts. For example, when we preach the cross, we should be those who can impart the life of the cross to other people. What pains me greatly is, that although many are now preaching the cross, the hearers do not seem to receive the life of God. People listen to our words; they appear to approve and gladly receive; yet the life of God is not present.

How often as we proclaim the substitutionary death of the cross, people may know the meaning and reason for such a death and may appear as though deeply moved at the moment; nevertheless, we do not witness the grace of God working in their midst and causing them to really receive the life of regeneration. Or, as another example, we may preach on the co-death aspect of the cross. We explain its teaching so plainly and persuasively that some people immediately commence to pray and may even determine to instantly die with Christ so as to experience the victory over sin and self. As time passes, however, we fail to notice in them the abundant life of God.

Such imperfect results give me much anguish. It drives me to humble myself before God and seek for His light. Now if you share the same experience, I would wish you to join me in sorrowing before the Lord and repenting together of our failure. What is lacking today are men and women who truly preach the cross, and who especially preach it in the power of the Holy Spirit.

In this connection, then, let us read the following portion from the word of God: "And I, brethren, when I came unto you, came not with excellency of speech or of wisdom, proclaiming to you the testimony of God. For I determined not to know anything among you, save Jesus Christ, and him crucified. And I was with you in weakness, and in fear, and in much trembling. And my speech and my preaching were not in persuasive words of wisdom, but in demonstration of the Spirit and of power" (1 Cor. 2.1-4).

In this passage we can discern the outline of three things: one, the message which Paul preaches; two, Paul himself; and three, how Paul proclaims his message.

One: The Message Which Paul Preaches

The message which Paul preaches is Jesus Christ

and Him crucified. His subject is the cross of Christ or the Christ of the cross. He knows this one matter — and nothing else. What a tremendous loss it will be to our audience as well as to ourselves if we forget the cross and do not make it and its Christ our one and only theme. I trust we are not among those who do not preach the cross at all.

Hence, in the light of this Scripture passage, our message and our theme may indeed be most correct. But do we not have the experience that despite the correctness of our message, we do not impart life to people? Let me tell you, that though it is essential to preach the right message, our labor shall be half in vain if it does not result in people receiving life.

We must underscore the point that the objective of our work is for people to have *life*. We preach the substitutionary death of the cross in order that God may grant His life to those who believe. What is the use if they are merely excited and moved to repent (even approving of what we preach) but their sympathy is only skin deep and the life of God does not enter into them. They are still unsaved. So our objective is not in inducing men only to repent or to have their mind influenced, but to *impart the life of God* to them that they may be saved. Even when we preach to the believer the deeper truth concerning the co-death of the cross, we must have the same objective in view.

Now it is rather easy to cause people to know and to understand a given matter. It really is not hard to persuade people to accept our teaching in their mind; believers and unbelievers alike, with some knowledge, can readily understand if the teaching is clearly explained to them. But for them to receive life and power and to experience what we preach, God has to work through us to dispense the more abundant life. We must never forget that *all the works we do are for the purpose of our being channels of God's life for that life to flow into people's spirits.* Therefore, in our having the correctness of both message and theme, we next need to make sure we are usable channels of God for transmitting life to other people.

Two: Paul Himself

The message Paul preaches is the cross of the Lord Jesus Christ. What he proclaims is not in vain since he is a living channel of divine life. With the gospel of the cross, he gives birth to many. Yet in preaching the word of the cross, what about himself? He says this: "I was with you in weakness, and in fear, and in much trembling." He *himself* is a crucified person! Let us see that it requires a crucified person to preach the word of the cross. Here Paul has absolutely no confidence in himself. His weakness, fear and much trembling—his looking upon himself as totally useless without any self-reliance—are the sure signs of his being a crucified one. "I have been crucified with Christ," Paul once declared (Gal. 2.20). He further said this: "I die daily" (1 Cor. 15.31). It takes a dying Paul to proclaim the crucifixion. Without the true dying of self, the life of Christ is not able to flow out from him. It is relatively easy to preach the cross, but to be a crucified person in the preaching of the crucifixion is not. If we are not crucified men and women, we cannot preach the word of the cross; no one will receive the life of the cross through our preaching unless we are so crucified. To speak quite frankly, he who does not know the cross experientially is not fit to preach the cross.

Three: How Paul Proclaims His Message

Paul's message is the cross, and he himself is a crucified person. In the preaching of the cross, he adopts the way of the cross. A crucified person preaches the message of the cross in the spirit of the cross. How often what we preach is indeed the cross; but our attitude, our words and our feelings do not seem to bear witness to what we preach. Much preaching of the cross is not done in the spirit of the cross! Paul wrote to the Corinthian believers that he "came not with excellency of speech or of wisdom when proclaiming" to them "the testimony of God." The testimony of God here refers to the word of the cross. Paul did not use lofty words of wisdom in proclaiming the cross but came in the spirit of the cross: "My speech and my preaching were not in persuasive words of wisdom, but in demonstration of the Spirit and of power." Such is truly the spirit of the cross.

The cross is the wisdom of God, though to unbelieving men it is foolishness. When we proclaim the "foolish" message, we must assume the "foolish" way, adopt the "foolish" attitude, and use the "foolish" words. The victory of Paul lies in the fact that he is indeed a crucified person. He can therefore proclaim the cross with the attitude as well as the spirit of the cross. He who has not experienced crucifixion will not be filled with the spirit of the cross; and consequently he is not fit to proclaim the message of the cross.

Having seen the experience of Paul, does it not tell us the cause of our failure? The message we preach may be right, but let us examine ourselves in the light of the Lord, discerning whether we really are crucified men and women. With what kind of spirit, words and attitude do we preach the cross? Oh! May we deeply humble ourselves in the face of these questions so that God may be gracious to us and that others listening to us may receive life.

Failure of people to receive life must be the failure of the *preachers*! It is not that the word has lost its power; it is men who have failed. Men have hindered the outflowing of the life of God, and not that the word of God has lost its effectiveness. People who do not have the *experience* of the cross and hence lack the *spirit* of the cross are unable to impart the *life* of the cross to others. How can we give to other people what we ourselves do not have? Unless the cross becomes our life, we cannot impart that life to others. The failure of our work is due to the fact that we are eager to preach the cross without that cross being within us. He who truly knows how to preach must have first preached the word to himself. Otherwise the Holy Spirit will not work through him.

The word of the cross which we so often proclaim is actually not ours but is borrowed — it is gleaned from books or from searching the Scriptures with our brain power. People with clever minds and those who are used to preaching are particularly prone to such danger. I am afraid that all their research, study, reading, and hearing talks on the mystery of the cross in its various aspects is for *other people* and not first for themselves. Consistently thinking of other people and neglecting our own lives will eventually result in spiritual famine!

In delivering the message, we try to present what we have heard and read and thought in an earnest and thorough manner. We may speak so clearly and logically that the mind of those in the audience may seem to understand it all. Nevertheless, though in understanding they do understand, there is not that compelling power to cause them to seek after that which they understand. It is as if knowing the theory of the cross is for them enough. Because of us, they stop with the knowledge of the cross without proceeding on to obtain what the cross will give to them—that is to say, the experience of the cross. Or perhaps the preacher well knows the art of mass psychology and so he speaks eloquently and earnestly. He may even advise the audience not to be satisfied with merely understanding what they have heard but to seek for experience as well. Yet, though his listeners may be temporarily stirred, they nonetheless fail to receive life. What they possess remains theory, it does not become experience.

Let us therefore never be self-satisfied, thinking that our eloquence can sway the audience. Although they may be stirred momentarily, let us realize that what they get from us are simply thoughts and words. Failure to impart life contributes absolutely *nothing* to men's spiritual walk. What is the use in giving peo-

ple only thoughts and words? I pray this will pene-
trate deeply into our hearts and cause us to reflect on
the vanity of our former works!

As we have seen, then, the two chief reasons for
our not imparting life while preaching the cross are:
(1) we ourselves do not have the experience of the
cross, and (2) we do not preach the word of the cross
in the spirit of the cross.

Reason for Failure in Messages of the Cross

Men and women who have not been crucified cannot and are unfit to, proclaim the word of the cross.
The cross we preach to others should first crucify us.
The word we preach should first burn itself deeply
into our life so that our life is the living message. The
cross we proclaim ought not just be a message. We
ought to let the cross live out of us daily. Then what
we preach will be more than a message but a kind of
life which we daily exhibit. Then we shall be able to
impart this life to others as we preach.

"My flesh is meat indeed," declared Jesus, "and
my blood is drink indeed" (John 6.55). When we exercise faith to draw upon the cross of the Lord Jesus, it
is as though we are eating His flesh and drinking His
blood. In such spiritual exercise, eating and drinking
are not mere words. For as in the natural realm, after
we have eaten and drunk, we digest what we have
taken in so that it becomes part of us—that is to say,
it becomes our life. Our failure lies in the fact that we
too often only use our intellect to examine God's
word and only take what we have read in books and

heard from teachers or friends as our message, using our minds, then, to organize the resultant material. Though we have many good thoughts and topics, and though our audience may listen very attentively and with interest, our work ends there, since we are unable to impart the life of God to them. The word we preach is indeed the cross, but we cannot share the life of the cross with others. All we have done is to communicate to them some thoughts and ideas. Do we not know that what people lack is not good thoughts but life?

Life

We cannot give what we do not have. If all we have is thought, we can only give thought. If in our life we do not have the experience of co-death with Christ to overcome sin and self nor the experience of taking up the cross to follow the Lord and suffer with Him, and if our knowledge of the word of the cross is obtained through people's pens and mouths but we have not experienced it ourselves, then it is certain we cannot impart life; all we can do is instill the *idea* of the life of the cross in people's minds. Only when we ourselves are transformed by the cross and have received its spirit as well as its life are we able to impart the cross to other people.

The cross ought to do its deeper work in our lives daily that we may have real experiences of the victory as well as the sufferings of the cross. Then as we proclaim it, our life will spontaneously be diffused in our words, and the Holy Spirit can flow out *His life* through our life to water the parched lives of the audience.

Man's thought, word, eloquence and argument can only stir up the human soul, since these reach to the soulical part of man. They merely excite man's emotion, mind and will. Life, however, may reach man's *spirit*; and all the works of the Holy Spirit are done in our spirit—that is, in our inward man (see Rom. 8.16; Eph. 3.16). As we in our spiritual experience let flow our life in the spirit, the Holy Spirit will send forth His life to the spirits of others and cause them to receive either regenerated life or the life more abundant.

How vain it is if we try to save sinners or build up saints by using psychology, eloquence and theory. Although judging by outward appearance what we say may be quite attractive, we know the *Holy Spirit is not working with us.* If the Holy Spirit is not working with His authority and power behind the words we speak, the hearers will undergo no change in their lives. Though they may sometimes make up their mind or strongly determine in their will, all these are merely excitement in the soul. Because there is no life behind our words, there is no power to cause others to receive what we do not possess. Having life is having power. Unless we allow the Holy Spirit to flow out of our life to reach the spirit in man, people cannot receive the life of the Holy Spirit and can have no power to practice what we have preached. What we seek for is therefore not the persuasiveness of words but the life and power of the Holy Spirit.

The life which we mention here refers to the word

of God which we experience in our walk or the message which we have experienced before proclaiming it. The life of the cross is the life of the Lord Jesus. We must know our message in experience. The teaching which we know is solely a teaching until we allow it to work in our lives so that the teaching we know becomes a part of our experience and an integral element in our daily walk. Then the teaching is not mere doctrine but is the very stuff of our life—just as the food we have eaten has become flesh of our flesh and bone of our bones. We become a *living* teaching and a *living* word; and what we preach is no longer simply an idea which we know but is our real life. This is the meaning of being "doers of the word" according to the Biblical sense.

We often misunderstand the word "do." We take it to mean that after we have heard and known the word of God we must try our best to do what we have heard and known. But this is not the meaning of "do" in the Bible. True, we need to will to do what we have heard. Yet the "do" of the Scriptures is not the doing with our own strength, it is instead allowing the Holy Spirit to *live out* through us the word of the Lord which we know. It is a kind of life, not just a kind of works. And in having the life, we will quite naturally have the works. But to produce a few works cannot be deemed fulfilling the "do" of the Bible. We ought to exercise our will to cooperate in life with the Holy Spirit so that we may live out what we know, thus imparting life to other people.

By looking at the Lord Jesus, we shall learn the lesson. "Even so must the Son of man be lifted up;

that whosoever believeth may in him have eternal life" (John 3.14b,15). "And I, if I be lifted up from the earth, will draw all men unto myself. But this he said, signifying by what manner of death he should die" (John 12.32,33). The Lord Jesus must be crucified before He could draw all men to himself to receive spiritual life. He himself must die first, having the experience of the cross working in Him both within and without so that He becomes in reality a crucified One. And thus will He have the power to draw all men to himself.

Now no disciple can be higher than his master. If our Lord must himself be lifted up and crucified in order for all men to be drawn to Him, ought not we who lift up the uplifted Christ also be lifted up and crucified so as to draw men to Him? The Lord Jesus was lifted up on the cross for the sake of giving spiritual life to men; likewise, if we desire to cause people to have spiritual life, we too must be lifted up on the cross so that the Holy Spirit may flow out His life through us as well. Since the source of life is from the cross, must not the channels of life also give life via the cross?

The Channels of Life

We have already mentioned how our work is to impart life to people. But in ourselves we have no life to give that people may live and be nourished. For we are not the source, we are merely channels of life. The life of God flows through us and from us. Since we are channels, we must not be blocked by anything lest, like water that is clogged in its channel, the life of God cannot pass through us. The work of the cross is to open us up—to rid us of all that belongs to Adam and the natural order so that others may receive the life of the Holy Spirit. By being filled with the Holy Spirit, our spirit is able to bear the cross of Christ continuously. As a result, our life becomes the life of the cross (on this we shall explain more later). And once filled with the Holy Spirit and possessing the life of the cross, we will then be used by God's Spirit to have issued from us that life of the cross to the people around us. For if we really are full of the Spirit due to the deeper work of the cross in us, we will spontaneously diffuse life in our conversation and our talk—whether private or public—so as to enrich those with whom we have contact. This does not require any self-effort or self-fabrication, but should be something most natural. And this thus fulfills what the Lord Jesus declares in John 7.38: "He that believeth on me . . . from within him shall flow rivers of living water."

This verse just quoted includes a number of thoughts. "From within him" or "out of his belly" (AV) requires that the belly be first emptied through the perfect work of the cross. It also implies that his belly must be filled with the living water of the Holy Spirit. The life in him is not only for his own need. It is so abundant and full that it flows out as rivers of living water to supply other people.

We need to pay special attention to the word "flow" here. Such a term does not suggest the use of platform tactics, a certain tone of voice, some profound psychology, some eloquence, argument or learning. Although all these may at times be helpful, they themselves are neither the living water nor the mechanism by which the living water issues forth. To "flow" suggests something most natural; it requires no human effort but simply follows the grade. There is no need to depend on eloquence or argument. By our faithfully proclaiming the word of Jesus' cross, people will receive the life which they lack. The life and power of the Holy Spirit appears to flow naturally through our spirit. Otherwise, no matter how passionately we preach, our audience will listen passively. And even if sometimes they may seem to pay full attention and may seem to understand and be moved, nevertheless, what we say can only draw a praise from their mouths without giving them the life and power to do what they hear. May we be the channels of God's life today.

To be channels we must have experience, or else the Holy Spirit will not work with us; for the work we do after receiving the power of the Holy Spirit carries with it the nature of testimony (see Luke 24.48,49). As a matter of fact, all our works bear witness to the Lord. He who testifies cannot testify to what he has not seen. Even the word of the hearer is not sufficient evidence. No one can testify without personal experience. To put it even more candidly, the one who has no experience of what he proclaims is a *fake* witness! And because of this the Holy Spirit refuses to work with such individuals.

Still another thing we ought to know is that when the Holy Spirit works (and even for that matter, when the evil spirit works), it is required that *man* be the outlet of the power. In case we have not experienced what we proclaim, the Holy Spirit cannot use us to be His channel to transmit His life to the heart of other people.

Hence may the cross which we proclaim crucify us on it! May we bear the cross we preach! May we first receive the life which we intend to impart to others! May the cross which we proclaim be that which we experience daily in our lives! For if our message is to produce eternal effect, it must first become the food of our soul. Through the trials of daily living it is burned into our very being so that we bear the mark of the cross in our every action. Those who bear, branded in their body, the marks of the Lord Jesus (Gal. 6.17) can alone proclaim Him. Oh, let me remind you that sudden thought or knowledge obtained from books and study may please the audience temporarily, but it will leave no permanent impression. If our work is simply for human appreciation, then we have already done our duty by presenting mental and emotional source materials. Fortunately, though, our work is not for such purpose!

The Success of the Apostle

The message of the cross has deeply influenced Paul. His life is clearly a manifestation of the life of the cross. He not only preaches the cross, he lives it. The cross he proclaims is that with which he has lived daily. So that when he speaks for the cross, he is able to add to his preaching his own experience and testimony. He knows the substitutionary death of Christ on the one hand, and on the other hand he takes the cross of the Lord Jesus as his own cross experientially. He can declare at one moment, "I have been crucified with Christ" (Gal. 2.20) and at the same time can declare this: "Far be it from me to glory, save in the cross of our Lord Jesus, through which the world hath been crucified unto me, and I unto the world" (Gal. 6.14). His gentleness, patience, weakness, tears, sufferings, and chains—all of these express the life of the cross. Because he lives the cross, he is fit to preach it. People often say so and so can talk but cannot walk. Who knows but what in actuality he who does not walk cannot talk? Since Paul lives out the gospel in his life, he is able to beget many spiritual children by the gospel. Having the life of the cross, he can "reproduce" the cross in the hearts of others.

The Cross and Its Messenger:
Personal Experience

In reading 2 Corinthians 4 we come to know the inner experience of this servant of the Lord. The secret to all Paul's works is found in this fragment: "So then death worketh in us, but life in you" (v.12). He died daily; he allowed the death of the cross to work deeply in him so that others might have life. Whoever does not know the death of the cross does not have the life of the cross for other people. Paul was willing to be in the place of death that others might receive life through him. Only the one who dies can give life. But how, Lord, to die?

What is the real meaning of this death? This death is more than death to sin, to self, and to the world. It is deeper than all these. This death is the spirit which our Lord Jesus exhibited when He was crucified on the cross. He does not die for His own sins, since He has none. Let us recognize that His cross declares His holiness. He is crucified wholly for the sake of *others*. Hence His death is due to His obedience to God's will. And such is the meaning of the death mentioned here. Thus we need to be delivered to death not only for our own sake that we may die to sin, self and the world, but also for the sake of obeying the Lord Jesus in enduring the hostility of sinners daily.

Yes, we ought to let the death of the Lord so work in us that we may have real experience of dying to self and arrive at the state of holiness. But we should equally let the Holy Spirit do a deeper work in us by the cross so as to cause us to live it out. We must know the *life* of the cross as well as its death. Having the death of the cross, we die to sin and the old Adamic walk; but having the life of the cross, we daily live in the spirit of the cross. This means that in our everyday walk we exhibit the Lamb-spirit of the Lord Jesus in suffering silently: "[Jesus] when he was reviled, reviled not again; when he suffered, threatened not; but committed himself to him that judgeth righteously" (1 Peter 2.23). This death is a step deeper than death to sin and self and the world. May the cross become our life! May we become a living cross! May we magnify the cross in all things!

The reason why Paul is able to impart life to people is because for him to live is the cross. He not only draws on the death of the cross negatively to eliminate what comes from Adam, he also takes the cross positively as his life and lives it out daily. Each day he apprehends the meaning of the cross of the Lord Jesus, and each day he exhibits the Lamb-life of the Lord Jesus: "Always bearing about in the body the dying of Jesus, that the life also of Jesus may be manifested in our body" (2 Cor. 4.10). He is willing to be "always delivered unto death for Jesus' sake, that the life also of Jesus may be manifested in [his] mortal flesh" (v.11). In his experience, therefore, Paul may be "pressed on every side, yet [he is] not straitened; perplexed, yet not unto despair; pursued, yet not forsaken; smitten down, yet not destroyed" (vv.8, 9). He allows the death of the Lord Jesus to "work" in his life (v.12).

A death that can work must be a "working death"—the life of death, even the life of the cross. For the sake of the Lord Jesus, Paul is ready always to be delivered to death. Notwithstanding unpleasant words, high-handed attitudes, cruel persecution, or unjustified misunderstanding, he is quite willing to bear them all for the Lord's sake. Paul will not open his mouth when he is delivered to death. Like his Lord who could ask the Father to send twelve legions of angels to help Him, he will under no such circumstances adopt man's way to avoid these unpleasantries. He would rather have the "living death" of Jesus—the life and spirit of the cross—worked in him so as to show forth the spirit of the cross in all his dealings. He reckons the cross as all powerful, because it enables him to be willing for the sake of the

Lord Jesus to be delivered to death and to suffer persecutions and hardships of the world.

How very deep the cross has worked in Paul's life! Yet how good it would be if we too would bear in our bodies the dying of Jesus! Who is the person today who is able to tell the Lord that he is willing to die, willing not to resist when he is put under all sorts of opposing and grievous circumstances? Yet if we desire other people to have the cross, we must let that same cross govern our own walk first. For it is only as the cross is allowed to burn into our own heart through the fire of sufferings and adversities that we shall be able to reproduce it in the hearts of other people. In other words, the life of the cross is that life which truly practices the Lord's sermon on the mount (see Matthew chapters 5-7, especially 5.38 with 44).

The text in 2 Corinthians 4 tells us plainly that we are not just preaching, we are manifesting the life of the Lord Jesus (vv.10,11). We are to let this life flow out from us. It is only when we bear in our bodies the dying of Jesus by our always being ready for Jesus' sake to be delivered to death that we are able to manifest the spirit of the Lamb of Calvary in the things we suffer for Him—whether such things be in respect to our name, our soul, or even our physical body. In so doing, there issues forth from us the life of Christ (vv.10,11). How sad, though, that we too often take the easy road, not realizing that there is no short cut to the manifestation of the life of the Lord Jesus.

"So then death worketh in us, but life in you" (v.12). The "you" here refers to the Corinthian believers together with all the Christians elsewhere.

They are Paul's audience. Since the dying of Jesus has worked in his experience, he is able to cause the life of Jesus to work in his audience too so that they might have spiritual life. The word "life" employed here is *zoe* in the original Greek—meaning spiritual life, the highest life. What Paul can offer to men is not merely his speech, thought, and a wooden cross; he offers to them the spiritual life of the Lord Jesus himself. This spiritual life can work in them until they shall arrive at the goal of the message which Paul preaches to them. This is not an empty verbal exercise, but is an operation of the supernatural life and power of God that makes entrance into the parched spirit of his audience, thereby causing them to receive the life of the cross which the apostle of God proclaims. We must reach this aim in our preaching of the cross or else never be satisfied until it is so.

To sum up, then, all who do not live the cross as Paul did can hardly expect to obtain the result which Paul had. If we ourselves are not crucified men and women, we will not be able to impart life to people in the preaching of the cross.

The Cross and Its Messenger: The Way of Proclaiming

We know not only that Paul is himself a crucified person in the preaching of the cross, but also that he preaches the cross in the spirit of the cross. In *ordinary times*, he is a crucified person; in *times of preaching*, he remains a crucified person, because he uses the spirit of the cross to preach the cross. He is a

man whose life experience has been one of being crucified with Christ. When he proclaims the cross, he
does not rely on his "excellency of speech or of wisdom" (1 Cor. 2.1, 4); for Paul fully realizes that these
are not good assets for his being a channel of God's
life. What he depends on instead is the "demonstration of the Spirit and of power." Only in this manner
is the word of the cross proclaimed with the proper
attitude.

So far as the genius and experience of Paul are
concerned, he is well able to announce the truth of the
cross in persuasive speech and with clever arguments.
He can present the tragic cross so movingly as to at-
tract great attention. He can develop the mystery of
the cross by using all kinds of suitable parables and
perceptive observations. He can also quote Scripture
to support the philosophy of the cross so that people
may understand the various aspects of the substitutionary death and co-death on the cross. All this Paul
is more than able to do. But he will not do so. His
heart refuses to rely on these abilities because he
knows these will never impart life to people. He is
fully aware that if he should depend on these assets he
would be preaching the word of the cross with "cross-
less" means. In the eyes of the world, the cross is
something humbling, lowly, foolish and despicable.
Yet this is exactly what the cross is. To preach it with
excellent speech and the wisdom of the world is totally contradictory to its spirit and can therefore be of
no avail. Paul is willing to deny his natural ability and
take the attitude and spirit of the cross in its preaching; consequently, God can greatly use him.

Every one of us has natural talent—some with more, others with less. After we have had some experience of the cross, we tend at first to depend on our natural gifts to proclaim the cross which we have newly experienced. How eagerly we expect our audience to adopt the same view and share in the same experience. Yet somehow they are so cold and unreceptive, falling short of our anticipation. We do not realize that we are rather new in our experience of the cross, and that our natural good talents need also to die with Christ. Are we ignorant of the fact that the cross must so work in us that not only should it be manifested in our lives but also be expressed in our works? But before we reach this more matured state, we usually look at our natural talent as harmless and very profitable in kingdom service. Hence why not use it? Not until we discover that the work done by relying on natural ability can only please men for a time but does not impart to their spirit the *actual* work of the Holy Spirit do we finally acknowledge how inadequate is our beautiful natural talent and how necessary it is that we seek for greater divine power. How many are those who proclaim the cross in their own power!

I do not say that these people have no experience of the cross; they no doubt have such experience. Neither would I imply that they openly state they will rely on their own gift and power to do the work. On the contrary, they may spend time in prayer, asking for God's blessing and the help of the Holy Spirit. They may even be aware to a certain extent of how undependable they themselves are. Yet all this does not help them much if in the *deep recesses of their heart* they are still self-reliant and confident that their eloquence or analysis, their thoughts and illustrations cannot fail to move people! The fact of our being crucified is expressed in helplessness, weakness, fear and trembling. In short, crucifixion spells death. Consequently, if we manifest the life of the cross in our daily lives, we must also exhibit the spirit of the cross in the *Lord's work*. We must always deem ourselves as helpless; in the Lord's service we must be in fear and trembling for our own sakes lest we rely on ourselves. In such a state we will no doubt depend on the Holy Spirit, and thus we shall produce fruit.

The least amount of self-reliance will unquestionably take away our reliance on the Holy Spirit. Only people who have been crucified know and are willing to know how to depend on the Spirit of God and His power. Paul, for instance, has himself been crucified with Christ; hence, when he works, he exhibits fully the spirit of the cross without any self-dependence. Because he uses the way of the cross to proclaim the Savior of the cross, the Holy Spirit and His power support Paul's testimony. May we say with our brother Paul: "Our gospel came not unto you in word only, but also in power, and in the Holy Spirit" (1 Thess. 1.5). For though we may speak movingly, what is the use if the Holy Spirit is not working behind our words? May we therefore not esteem our natural ability but be willing to lose everything that we may have the power of the Spirit of God.

Here lies the key to the fruitfulness or unfruitfulness of an evangelist. Sometimes we notice two preachers of the gospel. Their presentation and expression may be exactly the same. But one is used by God to bear much fruit, whereas the other—though what he says is spiritual and Scriptural and the audience appears to be most attentive—does not obtain any fruit and nothing seems to happen afterwards. It is not hard for us to discover the reason. I may say from my own observation that one of them is a truly crucified person who has had spiritual experience, but that for the other the entire presentation of the gospel is merely an idea. He who only possesses ideas cannot preach the cross in the way of the cross. But as he who possesses the life of the cross announces with his spirit the experience he possesses, he will have the Holy Spirit working with him.

Now some people may be more eloquent and more apt to analyze and to use illustrations; nonetheless, if they do not have the actual working of the cross in their lives, the Holy Spirit will not work with them. What they lack is the deeper operation of the Holy Spirit in them so that when they proclaim the gospel, the Holy Spirit will work with them and flow forth His life from them. They need to see that even despite the fact that at times the Lord *may* use their natural abilities, the *source* of any fruitfulness does not lie there. Whatever work is done by depending on natural life is mostly vain; but work performed in the power of the supernatural life bears much fruit.

Let us read another Scripture passage to help us understand what is the difference between depending on natural life and depending on supernatural life. "Verily, verily, I say unto you, Except a grain of wheat fall into the earth and die, it abideth by itself alone; but if it die, it beareth much fruit. He that loveth his life loseth it; and he that hateth his life in this world shall keep it unto life eternal" (John 12.24,25).

Here the Lord Jesus reveals the principle of fruit bearing: the grain of wheat which is sown must first *die* before it will bear much fruit. Hence death is the indispensable process for fruit bearing. The fact of the matter is, death *is* the only way to bear fruit. How we ask the Lord for greater power that we may bear more fruit; but the Lord tells us that we need to die, that we must have the experience of the cross if we desire the power of the Holy Spirit. Frequently in our attempt to achieve Pentecost we bypass Calvary, not realizing that without our being crucified and thus losing all belonging to the natural, the Holy Spirit cannot work with us to gain many people. Here is the spiritual principle: die, and *then* bear fruit.

The very nature of bearing fruit proves what we have stated before: the purpose of work is that people may receive life. This grain of wheat simply died, with the result that it produced many other grains. All these many grains now have life; but the source of the life they obtained was the *dead* grain of wheat. If we are truly dead, we will be the channels of God's life to transmit that life to other people. Hence this life is not a matter of vain terminology but has the power of God issuing forth from us to cause people to have life.

The fruit which this grain of wheat bears is manifold. Jesus said, "*Much* fruit"—that is to say, *many* grains. When we are bound up in our own life, we may gain one or two persons by exerting the utmost of our strength (and thus I do not imply here that we absolutely cannot save anyone). But if we die as the grain of wheat dies, we shall gain "much fruit." Wherever we go, and sometimes by merely dropping a word or two, people will be saved or edified. Let us therefore expect to bear much fruit.

But what does this phrase "fall into the earth and die" really mean? By reading the succeeding words which the Lord utters here, we may readily understand: "He that loveth his life loseth it; and he that hateth his life in this world shall keep it unto life eternal" (12.25). In the Greek original, two different words are used for the several times "life" is mentioned here. One Greek word *psuche* has reference to the soul life or natural life; the other word *zoe* signifies the spirit life or supernatural life. Hence what the Lord is actually saying here is: "He that loveth his soul life loseth the spirit life; and he that hateth his soul life in this world shall keep the spirit life unto eternity." To put it simply, we should deliver the soul life to death, just as the grain of wheat falls into the earth and dies; and then by our spirit life many grains will come forth and be kept to eternity. How we long to bear much fruit, yet we do not know how to let the soul life die and the spirit life live.

Soul life is our natural life. It is this soul life which enables our flesh to live. It is therefore the life factor of the natural man. A person's natural endowment belongs to the soul—such elements as our will, strength, emotions, thought, and so forth. These things which all natural lives share in common are accessories of the soul life. Our cleverness, reasoning, eloquence, affection, and ability belong to the soul life. The spirit life, though, is the life of God. It is not an evolvement from any part of the soul life but is a life especially given to us by the Holy Spirit when we believe in the finished work of the cross of the Lord Jesus and are saved. God is then in us to quicken this spirit life so that it may grow and thus become the power of all our good deeds and works. It is the will of God for Him to put our soul life in the place of death* (note, however, that this is different from the death prescribed in 2 Corinthians 4).

How frequently the power for our work comes from our natural endowment or soul life! How we depend on our eloquence, wisdom, knowledge, ability and so forth. Yet the most serious of all is that the strength we use in preaching proceeds from our soul life. We are using our *natural* strength, and this will greatly lessen our fruits. When we serve, we do not know how to draw upon the power of the spirit life; in fact, we often mistake soul life for spirit life. And thus we find ourselves depending on our natural strength. Not until we have exhausted the natural strength in our body do we then begin to rely on the power of the spirit life. Yet sad to say, many do not even reach *this* stage of understanding, for when their

---

*The reader should understand that the author, as has been made clear in many of his other books, is not advocating the death or annihilation of the soul and its functions. He merely stresses the necessity of having our soul life, which is the self life, crucified. — *Translator*

bodily strength is drained they incorrectly conclude
that they can no longer work for God. Happily, however, some are more advanced in spiritual life: when
they become weak, they learn to rely on the power of
the Lord to go on. Yet if from the outset we really
know how to die to our natural (or soulical) strength
and to depend wholly upon the power of the spirit life
which God has put in us, we will *never* work in the
strength of the soul life whether we have or do not
have natural strength.

It pains me greatly when I realize how many of the
believers' works—no matter how zealous and whole-
hearted their works may be—are done in the realm of
the soul instead of these believers reaching forth to
the realm of the spirit to do them. How to differentiate the spirit power from soul power is hard to explain
in words. We can only comprehend it in our heart, although when we are instructed by the Holy Spirit we
will understand it more clearly in experience.

For the sake of helping some of the weaker children of God, we will attempt to discuss this problem
more, although for truly knowing it in experience we
must ask the Spirit of God to reveal it to us. The characteristics of soulical work may chiefly be classified in
three ways; one, natural talent; two, emotion; and
three, mind.

Natural Talent

This we have already touched upon somewhat.
Some people possess higher natural endowments than
most; they are just naturally more alert. Some are

very eloquent, able to present their arguments convincingly. Others have the ability of analysis, dissecting a problem and putting everything in good order. Others are physically strong: they can keep on working non-stop all day. And still others are highly capable in managing affairs. Now we readily realize that God does make use of man's natural talents; but in so being used by God, men tend to *rely* on their talents.

For instance, there may be one believer who is dull in speech but sharp in management while another believer may be eloquent but is without managing ability. If the Lord were to send both of them to preach the word of God, the first would no doubt pray much and depend on the Lord, for he knows how dull he is in speech. The second believer, though he also would pray and depend on the Lord, would not be as wholeheartedly dependent on the Lord as the first one, for a believer such as he would almost invariably rely on his eloquence somewhat. Or if the Lord were to ask them to do some errand, the first believer would not be as dependent on the Lord as the second. Our natural talent is the power of our soul life. We hardly notice how self-reliant and dependent on the power of the soul we are in our works of service. From God's viewpoint, *many* are the works done by soul power!

Emotion

Feelings of emotion arise either from within ourselves or for the sake of other people. Sometimes, due to the fact that those whom we dearly love are not yet saved or else they fail to arrive at the place we anticipate for them, we are greatly stirred up to exert our maximum effort to save or edify them. Such kind of work is usually unfruitful, however, because it is motivated by our natural affection. At other times, we may receive special grace from God. As a result, our heart is so full of light and gladness that we feel as though a warm fire were burning within us which gives us joy unspeakable. At that moment the presence of God is most manifested; and our soul is so excited as to arouse from within us many emotional functions. It is extremely easy to work for the Lord in such an atmosphere then. Our heart is overflowing; and we can barely refrain from telling people of the things of the Lord. Ordinarily we may know we should not talk too much, but due to our receiving special light we now talk incessantly concerning the things of God. Let us acknowledge that such kind of work arises mainly from our emotion. Only when our heart is filled with this "warm fire" and we feel ourselves as having ascended to the third heaven can we work. But if the Lord does not give such joy which can be felt in us, then immediately we become as people with an unbearable load who cannot take even one step. In such a state our heart is cold as ice, we have no emotional uplift, and we cannot preach the gospel. At that moment our inner life appears so cut and dried that we simply cannot work. And even were we to force ourselves to work, it would be so heartless in nature.

Hence from all this we can see that work for God is almost entirely controlled by our feeling. When such warm feeling as described earlier comes to us, we can fly high as an eagle; when such feeling is lacking, we can hardly crawl. Since feeling, excitement and affection belong to the emotional part of our being, all saints who are governed by these inner motions work by the power of their soul life. They have yet to deliver these to death and to work in the spirit.

Mind

Our work for the Lord is frequently affected or even governed by our mind. Sometimes, not knowing how to seek the will of God, we will take the thought of our mind as His will, and thus we are led astray. To decide one's walk by obeying the mind is very dangerous. If in preparing to speak we wrack our brain to develop many points and outline divisions, many responses, principles and parables, such speech ends up being very dead. Though it may stir up some interest in the audience, it does not impart life to people.

There is another function of the mind which I believe many servants of God have wrongly used—and that is the memory. How often we use our power of memory in preaching! We memorize what we have previously heard, and later on preach what we have by this means stored up in our mind. Sometimes we tell people the Bible teaching we have memorized; at other times we preach to people with our notes. All these are the work of the mind. Yet I do not wish to imply here that we ourselves have absolutely no experience of what we preach. Perhaps what we have known and memorized are indeed the lessons which God has taught us in the past, and hence we have actually experienced them. Nevertheless, if we deliver them out of memory or note-taking *alone*, they inescapably belong to the work of the mind.

Why do I say this? It is because a little while after we have had some experience in a certain truth, and though originally it did become our life, only the *knowledge* of this truth has been stored away in our brain. And if we subsequently use the power of memory to recall and to preach the truth which we had formerly experienced, our work remains in the realm of our mind. Now since mind and memory belong to the soul, our dependence on them means that we rely on the power of the soul life. We are still under the control of the natural life.

The above three characteristics are the more prominent of our soulical works. Such soulical works are not sins, nor are they totally ineffective in saving people; yet the fruits they produce are very limited. We ought to overcome these kinds of soulical works by depending on the cross. The Lord Jesus has taught us that our soulical, natural life should, like a kernel of wheat, fall into the ground and die. Speaking according to our *experience*, we quite naturally think highly of our talent, delight in our feeling, and trust in our thought. But our Lord tells us we must hate this soul life; otherwise, in loving it we will lose the power of that supernatural spirit life God has imparted to us. The death of the cross should work deeply in this area of our natures. We should be willing to deliver to the cross the soul life which we love, being willing to die with Christ in this respect to rid ourselves of the dependence on natural talent, feeling and thought so that we may hate this kind of work from the depth of our heart. As we are serving the Lord, we must reckon talent, feeling and thought as nothing. We hate this kind of power of the natural life and are ready to deliver it to the death of the cross.

If on the negative side we always maintain the attitude of uncompromisingly hating our soulical life, we shall learn experientially how to depend on the power of the spirit life and thus bear fruits to the glory of God.

The Way of a Crucified Person Proclaiming the Cross

Speaking on the practical side, whenever the Lord sends us to a certain place at a certain time to testify for Him, we need to rid ourselves anew of the inclination to love and to depend upon our natural life, and to be willing to set aside our emotion or feeling. Although sometimes we do not feel anything or we feel as cold as ice, we may kneel before the Lord and ask that the cross may do its deeper work in us so that we can *control* our feeling — be it cold or hot — in carrying out the command of the Lord. We may ask further that the Lord will strengthen our spirit. And as our soul life at that moment receives its fatal blow on the cross, the Lord will grant more grace to us. Even if we have already known the truth which we are to preach, we dare not draw it out from our brain and deliver it to people. Instead, we will humbly prostrate before

God, asking Him to quicken afresh the truth we already knew. And thus the truth will be impressed upon us anew so that what we speak is not merely the memory of our past experience but is something which we seem to newly experience in our life. In this way will the Holy Spirit with His power verify what we preach. It is best for us to wait before the Lord for a little while before we ever speak, allowing His word (or sometimes that which we already knew) to impress itself upon our spirit afresh. Even at times when we are pressed for time, the Lord is still able to imprint the message upon our spirit within a few minutes. Such experience requires the constant opening of our spirit to the Lord in our daily walk.

We must underline this point, because it is the key to our success or failure. In the case of a backslidden believer, if he is asked to speak of his past experience, he is able to do it by the power of memory and he may even speak attractively. But we all know that the Holy Spirit will not work through him. Yet let us see that the work which *we* do by the power of memory is not much different from the preaching or speaking of the backslidden. We ought quickly to recognize that the work which is done with the mind is frequently a waste of energy. For what comes merely out of the mind can only reach the mind of other people. It can never touch the spirit and give life. Old experience not freshly quickened is inadequate for new work. We must ask God to renew the old experience in our spirit.

This that we have just said is even more true when preaching the salvation of the cross to sinners. Perhaps we have been saved for decades. If we labor solely by the power of memory, will not our message be too old and too tasteless? But if we can see anew in our spirit the ugliness of sins and taste afresh the love of the cross, we shall be so touched by the compassion of Christ for sinners to believe in Him that we are able to portray the cross livingly before the people (see Gal. 3.1) for them to believe in Him. How can we ever move others with the love and compassion of Christ if we ourselves are so hard and cold! For perhaps while we are proclaiming the sufferings of the cross, our hearts are not in the least touched and melted by such sufferings!

We must therefore go before the Lord with our spirit opened so that His Holy Spirit may make His word and message pass through our spirit, causing us to be melted by His word before we ever deliver it. We must not depend on our feeling, natural talent or mind, but depend instead on the power of the Holy Spirit. Let His message impress itself upon the spirit of the audience as well as upon our spirit. Oh! Each time we preach we should be like Isaiah, who was always *burdened* with the prophecy before he ever prophesied. In reading Isaiah chapters 13 through 23, we will note that each prophecy is headed by the word "burden." This should be most meaningful for us. Every time we proclaim the word of God we must first receive in our spirit the burden of the message we are to deliver, as though we cannot be discharged of the burden until our work is done.

Furthermore, we ought to ask the Lord to give us burden so that the work we do will not come from our natural feeling, talent or mind. We should also experience what Jeremiah had experienced: "If I say, I will not make mention of him, nor speak any more in his name, then there is in my heart as it were a burning fire shut up in my bones, and I am weary with forbearing, and I cannot contain" (20.9). How can we be careless in proclaiming God's word? We must let His word first burn in our spirit so that we cannot but speak. Yet if we are not willing to deliver our soul life and its power to death, we will never receive afresh the word of God in our spirit.

If we as His servants wish to be used by God to save sinners and to revive saints—that is, to proclaim the word of the cross—we must let the cross first work in us: to make us, on the one hand, willing to deliver ourselves daily to death for the Lord's sake and on the other hand, willing to put the power of our soul life in the place of death—abhorring the strength which belongs to the natural life and placing no confidence in ourselves as well as in all which proceeds from self. Then shall we see the life of God and its power flowing into people's spirits through our words.

Nevertheless, in spite of all the preparations on the part of the evangelist or preacher himself, he may still sometimes fail. Yet it will not be due to a total failure on his part. And why? Because of the oppression and attack of Satan.

The Oppression and Attack of Satan

Satan hates the preaching of the word of the

cross. If we faithfully proclaim the Lord's cross, we will suffer opposition from him. He often assaults the messenger of the cross in the following ways. He may attack by weakening the latter's health—causing him to lose his voice or to encounter many physical dangers—or by oppressing his spirit to near suffocation. He may work in the environment to create misunderstanding, opposition, and even persecution. He may disturb the weather, hindering people from attending meetings. He may cause disorder or confusion in the meeting. He may incite the dogs to bark or the babies to cry. Sometimes he may work in the atmosphere, making the meeting heavy, suffocating, oppressive or gloomy. All these are the works of the enemy which a messenger of the cross must recognize.

Since we have such an enemy and may encounter such opposition, we ought to know the victory of the cross. What the Lord Jesus has there accomplished is more than solely solving the problem of the sinner. There He has pronounced the sentence of judgment upon Satan; there He has defeated the enemy: ". . . That through death he might bring to nought him that had the power of death, that is, the devil; and might deliver all them who through fear of death were all their lifetime subject to bondage" (Heb. 2.14b, 15)—"Having despoiled the principalities and the powers, [the Lord Jesus] made a show of them openly, triumphing over them in it" (Col. 2.15). The cross is where Satan has been overcome, for he has received the fatal blow there. We know that "to this end was the Son of God manifested, that he might destroy the works of the devil" (1 John 3.8). And where does this happen? The simple answer is: at the cross. We also know that the Lord Jesus came to "bind the strong man" (Matt. 12.29). And where again? Naturally, at Calvary's cross. We ought to realize that the Lord Jesus has won the battle on the cross. We must know—

The Victory of the Cross

We need to recognize that Satan is already a defeated foe. And hence we must not be defeated and the enemy must not conquer. Satan has no right to overcome again! Except for a total defeat of himself, he should not have anything. Let us therefore lift up the victory of the cross both before and after we see the work of Satan. Let us praise aloud the victory of Christ. Before we begin to work, we can declare before the Lord: "Praise the Lord, for He has overcome! Christ is the Overcomer! Satan is already defeated! The enemy is already destroyed! Calvary is victory! The cross is victory!" We may so declare this till in our *spirit* we know the Lord will again win the fight. We should stand on the ground of the cross, asking for victory as well as for the destruction of the works of the devil. We should ask God to cover us, and those who attend the meeting, with the precious blood of our Lord Jesus so that we will not be attacked by Satan but will overcome him. "And they overcame him [Satan] because of the blood of the Lamb" (Rev. 12.11).

Recently while I was laboring in southern Fukien Province, the devil frequently tried to oppress and assault me. Yet the Lord taught me in this experience that I should stand on the ground of the cross and praise Him. At times my spirit was deeply oppressed; I had no liberty, as though a weight of a thousand pounds was being pressed on my heart. At other times, upon entering the meeting hall, I felt the very air had been polluted by the works of the devil. Under such circumstances, and though I prayed most earnestly, I could not prevail. So I began to praise Christ for His victory on the cross: I boasted in the cross and derided the enemy, saying he could not work anymore for he was a defeated foe. Subsequently I felt truly liberated, and the atmosphere of the meeting was also changed. Praise the Lord, for the cross *is* victorious! Praise the Lord, for Satan *is* defeated! We should know how in prayer to exercise the various aspects of the victory of the cross against all the wiles, powers, and assaults of the enemy. Whenever there is opposition and any kind of confusion, we can declare the victory of Calvary's cross. Though we may not feel anything, yet by faith we claim its victory, and the enemy shall be defeated.

If we are really joined to the cross — allowing it to do a deeper work in our life and service, and trusting wholeheartedly in the victory of the cross — God will cause us to triumph everywhere. May God awaken us who are unprofitable servants to be workmen "that needeth not to be ashamed" (2 Tim. 2.15).

Written January 15, 1926,
in Amoy, China

2 | In Christ

We should never forget that all of us were sinners because we all were in Adam. Every one born of Adam inherited the nature of Adam. It took no effort when sinners for us to lose our temper, tell a lie, and so forth, since the life, nature and behavior of Adam flowed in us. Now the way of salvation for us was not in God making us good but in His saving us out of Adam and putting us in Christ. So that now, all which is of Christ flows into us. The Bible shows us that as soon as we are in Adam we sin, and that only as we are in Christ do we practice righteousness. May I remind ourselves that lurking in the secret place of many of our hearts lies an error: the thought of expecting God to change us. But God does not and never will do anything in us; instead, He will put us *in Christ.*

Our pattern of thought is that since the root of sin is in us, we must ask God—after we are saved—to eradicate our root of sin just as we ask a dentist to ex-

tract a painful tooth from our mouth. Perhaps some
people will even tell you and me that we must pray
and ask God to eradicate our root of sin. They may
perhaps also inform us that after a long time of
prayer they themselves have succeeded in this and
have thus attained holiness.

But let me hasten to tell you that if you expect
God to do such a thing to you as the eradication of
the root of sin, you will be disappointed, for God
would never do it. What the Bible shows us is that all
the works of God have been *accomplished in Christ.*
From the day on which Christ died, every spiritual
thing has been accomplished in Him. God can do no
more. So that if you ask God to do something like
this in you, He cannot do it. You can only receive
what He has *already* done in Christ.

All is in Christ. Do you expect in your prayer to
see some special light or hear some special voice saying to you that your particular sin is now being eradicated? Or do you look for a distinctive sensation to
fill you with joy? You may deem these things to be
good; in actuality, though, this shows your evil heart
of unbelief. For all that God does He does in
Christ—not in you. So that it is now no longer what
God will do in you but what God has done in Christ.
And by believing the latter, you will have it. You shall
only possess it by appropriating it in Christ.

Often when sick you think you will be well if only
God would touch you with His little finger. But God
has already healed you in Christ; He can do no more
in you. If you believe and appropriate it in Christ,

you shall indeed be sound and healthy. Are you thinking of victory? The victory of Christ alone is your triumph. Do you want to overcome the world? Again, it is Christ who has overcome the world. Or do you expect God to do something for you some day? Let me say once again, no, since God has already done everything for you in Christ. Hence victory is not a present-day affair, because Christ has *already* triumphed. May God grant us such a revelation that we may see *what we already have in Christ*. If we do not believe, we will receive nothing; but if we do believe, we have everything. In Christ are victory, justification, sanctification, forgiveness, and every other spiritual blessing. God can do no more for us. If we be in Christ, all which is Christ's is ours. It is not drawing out of Christ something to nourish us, but entering into Christ so as to allow what is already in Him to flow in us.

When we are baptized, we are baptized into Christ — not our merely being baptized in water but being baptized into Christ. According to the last clause in Romans 6.3 ("were baptized into his death"), the water of baptism spoken of in that verse points to death. But according to the first clause of the same verse ("were baptized into Christ Jesus"), the water also refers to Christ. Frequently we look to God for a cup of water. No, God wants us to enter into Christ. If we are clear on this point, we shall know that it is not a matter of we ourselves, nor our asking God to do something in us; it is instead Christ, and all things are in Him.

I. What We Have in Christ

"There is therefore now no condemnation to them that are in Christ Jesus" (Rom. 8.1). How can we not be condemned? By our being in Christ Jesus. Can you say to God, "I am a sinner, please forgive me and do not condemn me"? No, God cannot do it directly for you, He can only forgive you in Christ. You must not look at yourself; you must look at Christ. May I ask, How do you know you will not be condemned in the future? Can you rely on your experience you had at a certain time or on a certain day? Clearly you can only stand firm and sure on what the Scriptures say. And then neither I nor all the preachers of the world nor even God himself can refute you; and in this case, it is because the word of God states that "there is therefore now no condemnation to them that are in Christ Jesus."

"If any man is in Christ, he is a new creation: the old things are passed away; behold, they are become new" (2 Cor. 5.17 mg.). Does it say here how much I have changed? Not at all. It simply says if any man is in Christ, he is a new creation. Someone may assert that he had been a weak Christian for a number of years until later during a certain year in a certain month he was revived and thus he became a new creation. Of such a person I would ask this: What is the ground for your assertion that at such and such a time you became a new creation? The only true ground does not lie in the fact that in a certain hour of revival one became a new creation, but in what the word of

God has declared; namely, that if anyone is in Christ Jesus he is a new creation.

Perhaps someone will argue that despite what the Scriptures say of his being a new creation, as he looks at himself he does not seem to be very new. I would again answer with this: How many sinners and saints are lacking in faith! Let me encourage us all to kneel and pray: "God, I praise and thank You, Your word says that if any man is in Christ he is a new creation. I am in Christ, therefore I am a new creation." Whenever the temptation comes to you which declares you are still the old man, if you will but answer with the word of God which says that you are in Christ and therefore you are a new creation, Satan will beat a hasty retreat. Or if you simply stand on the side of God's word and pay no attention to such temptation, you will also gain the victory. For victory does not rely on feeling but on the word of God.

Let me reiterate once more the truth that God will not do anything in us. If He were to pull out our root of sin, we would have no need to trust Him thereafter. But God has accomplished all things in Christ in order that we may look to Him day by day. He cannot lie; what He says is true. And if we believe, it shall be ours. This is the secret of victory.

"To the praise of the glory of his grace, which he freely bestowed on us in the Beloved" (Eph. 1.6). God accepts us only in His Beloved One—even in Christ. None can be accepted by God outside of Christ, for God can only receive and accept us in Him.

"In whom [the Son of God's love] we have our redemption, the forgiveness of our sins" (Col. 1.4). To be redeemed and forgiven is something only found in Christ. Suppose a Christian has sinned and he asks God to forgive him. Do you know when God forgives him? Some say pray until there is peace in the heart, for this is the evidence of forgiveness. Are there not many who have committed many sins and yet their hearts are quite at peace? Are there not also many whose sins have been forgiven but they still feel unpeaceful? How utterly undependable is man's feeling. In case a Christian has sinned, how long will you tell him he must pray before he can receive forgiveness? Let it be known that over nineteen hundred years ago Christ had already borne your sins away: that you have already died in the death of Christ, and hence you have already received forgiveness. All is well if you simply appropriate what Christ has already accomplished for you. If you wait for God to do a new thing in you, you may have to pray until eternity comes. When we today ask God for forgiveness, we simply mean let the forgiveness that is already in Christ flow into us. We receive forgiveness because we believe God has already forgiven us in Christ. It does not depend on feeling.

"[Christ] who knew no sin [God] made to be sin on our behalf; that we might become the righteousness of God in him" (2 Cor. 5.21). We are justified because we are in Christ. It is not because we have done good works that God justifies us. God justifies us in His Son. If we wait until we are righteous before we will believe, we shall never believe.

"Unto the church of God which is at Corinth,

even them that are sanctified in Christ Jesus, called to be saints, with all that call upon the name of our Lord Jesus Christ in every place, their Lord and ours" (1 Cor. 1.2). Just as we are justified because we are in Christ, so also we are sanctified because we are in Christ. The great mistake many make is to assume that in a certain month on a certain day God grants them sanctification and so they are sanctified. May I tell you that if you today expect God to make you sanctified, you will never be sanctified. You can only appropriate what Christ has already accomplished for you.

We would rather be like the light in a car which comes from the little electricity stored in the car. But if we are in Christ, we will be like the light in a house. Though the electricity is not in the bulb, it flows into it; for as soon as the switch is opened, the connection is made and the light comes on. But when the switch is off and the connection is cut, the light goes out. Now inasmuch as we are joined to Christ, we have everything; but if there are interruptions, we shall be like a Gentile. There has never been any work done in us, since all has been done in Christ. We are but conductors.

"I am persuaded that neither death, nor life, nor angels, nor principalities, nor things present, nor things to come, nor powers, nor height, nor depth, nor any other creation, shall be able to separate us from the love of God, which is in Christ Jesus our Lord" (Rom. 8.38, 39 mg.). None of these things can separate us from the love of God because of one very important reason—this love is in Christ Jesus.

"In him [Christ] ye are made full" (Col. 2.10). Our being made full is not due to anything done in us but due to our being in Christ.

"The law of the Spirit of life in Christ Jesus made me free from the law of sin and of death" (Rom 8.2). We are made free not because of ourselves but because we are in Christ. Blessed is he who believes in this.

God "hath blessed us with every spiritual blessing in the heavenly places in Christ" (Eph. 1.3). This verse we may truly enjoy without end. Whatever spiritual blessing there is, it is in Christ. Having such a verse, you may continually say: "Thank and praise God, for He has given me every spiritual blessing in the heavenly places in Christ." To the extent that you believe in what God has said, to that extent will all He has said be real to you.

"In me [the Lord Jesus] ye may have peace" (John 16.33). Peace is not found outside of the Lord. As we are abiding in the Lord, we will have the peace of the Lord.

"If there is therefore any exhortation in Christ, if any consolation of love, if any fellowship of the Spirit, if any tender mercies and compassions" (Phil. 2.1). All is in Christ.

"I know a man in Christ" (2 Cor. 12.2). Here is a man in Christ, a man who is wholly in Him.

Oh, if we carefully read the Bible, we will not ask God to do anything in us. For in the event we expect Him to do something in us, we shall be disappointed not only today and tomorrow but even up to the day we depart from this world. In the natural realm, if the switch is off, how can one ever expect the light to shine? But as soon as the switch is on, the light instantly arrives. Even so, in the spiritual realm, without constantly believing in Christ, we will not have the victory. We need Christ every moment. In Him we have everything.

II. How To Be in Christ

(1) He who believes into Christ is in Christ. "For God so loved the world, that he gave his only begotten Son, that whosoever believeth on [Greek, *into*] him [Christ] should not perish, but have eternal life" (John 3.16). This is union. We believe into Christ.

(2) Having believed into Christ, we should also be baptized into Him. To be water baptized is to be baptized into Christ: "Are ye ignorant that all we who were baptized into Christ Jesus were baptized into his death?" (Rom. 6.3) As you are baptized in water, so you are baptized into Christ. If you were to put a copper coin into a bottle of sulphuric acid, the copper coin would disappear because it would be melted in the acid. Likewise, as you are baptized into Christ you become one with Him. This is faith.

(3) Of God are we in Christ (see 1 Cor. 1.30). It is God who baptizes us into Christ. With our believing into inwardly and our being baptized into outwardly, God joins us to Christ. And thus have we both righteousness, sanctification and redemption. We have no righteousness, but Christ is our righteousness. We have no sanctification, but Christ is our sanctification. We have no redemption, but He is our redemp-

tion. We shall see Christ in all things. May God take away our veil that we may see how perfect is the work which He has accomplished for us.

Hudson Taylor expended great effort in seeking for victory. He acknowledged that in spite of his constant asking, God had not given him victory. One day he read Christ's words in John 15.5: "I am the vine, ye are the branches." Instantly he received light. He knelt and prayed: "I am the most foolish person in the entire world. The victorious life which I seek is actually something I have already possessed. You *are* the branch, Jesus said, and not that you shall become a branch." For many years he asked to be joined to the tree like a branch, not realizing that he was already a branch joined to the tree. Not till then did he receive the revelation of God, and have real faith. Thereafter he lived a victorious life and accomplished great things for the Lord. Sometime later, he was asked to speak at the Keswick Convention in England, and such was the story he told there. And he said this: "I was defeated, so I sought for victory; but victory never came. But on the day I believed, victory did come."

Let us see that we do not try with effort to draw out the sap from the root to nourish us, for we are branches already joined to the tree. We need to be concerned for nothing except that we are branches. Let us not try to obtain something out of the tree, but simply believe that we are the branches. God has joined us to Christ the Tree. And whatever is Christ's is also ours. Believing, we have the victory.

We are baptized into Christ on the one hand and on the other hand we maintain contact with Him through the bread and the cup. In so doing, we allow His life to flow through us.

3 | The Power of Choosing

The Lord himself will give you a sign. Behold, a virgin shall conceive, and bear a son, and shall call his name Immanuel. Butter and honey shall he eat, when he knoweth to refuse the evil, and choose the good. (Is. 7.14,15)

In the marginal note for verse 15 we find this other translation: "Butter and honey shall he eat, that he may know to refuse the evil, and choose the good." Thus it is not after he knows to refuse the evil and choose the good that he eats butter and honey; rather, it is *because* he eats butter and honey that he shall know how to refuse the evil and choose the good.

We wish to learn somewhat more concerning the Lord Jesus Christ here. You know as well as I how perfect was the life of our Lord during His earthly days. In reading the four New Testament Gospels we observe how good and how perfect was the way our

Lord lived on earth. But from these four accounts alone we cannot find out *why* the Lord can live such a "super human" life or *why* He is so perfect or *why* He is such a Son of man. It is Isaiah 7.15 which tells us the reason why. Why does He know to refuse the evil and choose the good? Why does He know how to reject the world and choose the will of God? Why does He know to deny the glory of man and desire only the glory of God? All this is revealed in Isaiah.

We all agree that verse 14 ("A virgin shall conceive, and bear a Son, and shall call his name Immanuel") points to the Messiah, our Lord Jesus. Unfortunately, many overlook the very next verse. We ought to understand that not only verse 14 points to the Lord, verse 15 does also. Verse 15 declares that during His entire life He shall eat butter and honey. And that because He so eats throughout His life, He shall be *able* to choose the good and refuse the evil, He shall be *able* to obey God and seek God's glory, and shall be *able* to gain God's heart satisfaction.

What are the meanings of both butter and honey? Of all the flavors, that of butter is the richest. And of all things on earth, nothing is sweeter than honey. Hence butter stands for the richest and honey stands for the sweetest.

What does the Bible say is the richest thing? The grace of God (Eph. 1.7). What does it say is the sweetest? The love of God (S. of Sol. 2.3). God places the riches of His grace and the sweetness of His love before the Lord Jesus for Him to eat, and therefore He is able to obey God and choose His will, to refuse the evil and choose the good. For a few moments, then, I would like to dwell on how the Lord throughout His life ate butter and honey, and also how as a consequence He refused the evil and chose the good.

One: His Early Years (Luke 2.41-51)

When Jesus was twelve years of age, He went with His parents to Jerusalem to keep the feast of the Passover. After the days were fulfilled, His parents were returning; but the boy Jesus remained in Jerusalem. Later His parents came back to the city to find Him. Three days later they found Him in the temple. Then His mother said to Him, "Son, why hast thou thus dealt with us? behold, thy father and I sought thee sorrowing." In answering, the Lord did not say, "Knew ye not that I must do the will of God?" Instead He said, "Knew ye not that I must be in my Father's house [or, about my Father's business]?" Here the Lord had butter and honey.

At twelve years of age, Jesus already knew the Father. He had the heavenly butter and honey. Because He had the richest and sweetest, He was able to live in the will of God. If this had happened to us, we would probably have answered: "You go back to Nazareth and resume the work of carpentry and housekeeping, but I am not going. Let me stay in the temple." Yet our Lord did not answer this way. On the one hand, He gave His testimony; but on the other hand, He went down with His parents to Nazareth and obeyed them. He could make this difficult choice because He had tasted the riches and the sweetness of God.

Now the mother of Jesus was one of the best women in the world; at the same time, though, she was
also a "little" woman. Frequently the best people are
the least brainy. As we read the four Gospels we shall
find how Mary often disturbed the Lord. When the
wine failed at the marriage feast in Cana, she said to
Him, "They have no wine" (John 2.3). When the
Lord was teaching many people, she sent word to
Him that she wanted to talk to Him (Mark 3.31). Yet
the Scripture says: "He went down with them, and
came to Nazareth; and he was subject unto them."
This was the Lord's choice, which was something
difficult for man. He could have refused to return
and chosen to stay in the temple, but He would rather
choose returning home and living with Mary who had
little understanding. Because He had eaten butter and
honey, He was able to choose what was hard for man.

Two: Baptized with John's Baptism
(Matt. 3.13-17)

When John the Baptist saw Jesus coming to him,
he said: "Behold, the Lamb of God, that taketh away
the sin of the world!" (John 1.29) Again John said
this about Jesus: "He that cometh after me is mightier
than I" (Matt. 3.11). How much mightier? "Whose
shoes I am not worthy to bear," he had said (Matt.
3.11). The Lord Jesus was so great, and yet He came
to be baptized by John. Had we been in His place —
that is to say, in the place of His being so great even
from eternity as the King of the kingdom of heaven

— we would no doubt have been accompanied by all the pomp of our high position. Although we might never openly acknowledge it, it is easy for us to display our excellency. Our pride is something natural-born. We just love to exhibit our greatness before other people. But our Lord came to the river Jordan and received the baptism of John the Baptist.

Do you think it is easy to receive baptism from man? There was in Foochow an elderly sister. She was a good woman. At one time she knew she ought to be baptized, but she herself chose the person baptizing her. She respected certain brothers, but others she despised. She insisted on having one particular brother baptize her. One who has lived a better life on earth and who later seeks baptism seeks out a person whom he or she respects to do the baptizing.

Now our Lord was very special. He was so different that He surprised John the Baptist, who tried to stop Him by saying: "I have need to be baptized of thee, and comest thou to me?" What do you think the Lord said in reply? "Suffer it now: for thus it becometh us to fulfill all righteousness." He would rather come to the Jordan River and enter the water of death. He chose humility, and He chose death. And thus did He fulfill all righteousness. Actually righteousness is accomplished on the cross, but it was foreshadowed in the water of death for Jesus. He chose the good and refused the evil.

Have you ever thought how difficult it must have been for the Lord to have received the baptism of John the Baptist? For what might happen to His dignity in the world before the sinners, the publicans and the prostitutes? For were they not also receiving the baptism of John the Baptist? And when He himself had begun later to preach, He too proclaimed like John: "Repent ye, for the kingdom of heaven is at hand" (Matt. 4.17). His audience was the same as John's. A certain publican might therefore say: "Was He not one who was baptized with us that day? How can He now come to teach us today?" Another sinner might with equal justification declare: "He was baptized together with us on that day. How dare He come to teach us now?" How hard and undignified it must have been for Jesus.

In point of fact, later on this problem actually arose. For when the Lord and His disciples were in Judea baptizing people, some came to John and complained: "He that was with thee beyond the Jordan, to whom thou hast borne witness, behold the same baptizeth, and all men come to him" (John 3.26). This proves how they despised the Lord. The Lord indeed puts himself into this difficult position, but He chooses to do so because there is strength behind His decision. He has tasted the greatness of abundant grace and God's sweet love. He has eaten butter and honey. Having tasted the most abundant and the sweetest, He is able to take the lowliest place.

We also are able to humble ourselves and take the lowly place because we too have the butter and the honey. What the people of the world cannot do we Christians can, for we have the grace most abundant and the love most sweet.

Three: At the Time of Temptation
(Matt. 4.1-10)

Upon the Lord being baptized and coming up out of the water, the heaven was suddenly opened for Him and the Holy Spirit descended on Him as a dove. He then was led by the Spirit to the wilderness and was tempted by the devil for forty days and nights. Satan himself appeared to tempt Him, saying: "If thou art the Son of God, command that these stones become bread." Eating while hungry is no sin, but the Lord refused to eat here. The tempter aimed at enticing the Lord to do a thing according to His own will. He tried to lure Jesus into using His own way to satisfy His hunger. But the Lord retorted: "It is written, Man shall not live by bread alone, but by every word that proceedeth out of the mouth of God." He is willing to be hungry, and He is able to bear hunger. May I put it before you all today that if we wish to live as the Lord lived we must daily receive from heaven both butter and honey. The Lord is well able to turn stones into bread, but He has no need for it because He already has the butter and the honey.

Suppose a little pleasure, a little comfort or glory is at your fingertips? You can have it if you say yes, or you can have it without even saying anything. It is already within your sphere of influence. You may obtain it without effort. What will you do? Our Lord is not willing to turn a stone into bread, but how we hope we might be able to do it—and not turning merely one stone into bread but all the stones in the River Jordan as well!

How we long to exert our utmost strength for ourselves. This is because we have not had the butter and the honey of heaven. Had we eaten that way, we would be able to forsake what could likely be ours and let go what is at our fingertips. Only one kind of people in the world knows how to offer to God—they are those who experience the grace of God.

The temptation which Jesus suffered in the desert was not in one area alone. For Satan additionally said to the Lord: "If thou art the Son of God, cast thyself down." How marvelous it would be to fly down from heaven! Would not people immediately acknowledge Him as the Messiah? He could gain immense glory by the simplest of means. Yet the Lord would not do that. Again a third time Satan said to Him: "All things will I give thee, if thou wilt fall down and worship me." Is it not an easy thing to gain the whole world and all the glory therein by a surreptitious bow? Nevertheless, however good all the kingdoms of the world are, our Lord is able to forsake and deny because He has power in Him. He knows God in a way which is beyond us; He is filled with the Holy Spirit in a way that we are not; and He has tasted the abundance of grace and the sweetness of love to a degree that we do not experience.

Four: The Lord Reprimands Peter
(Matt. 16.21–23 mg.)

On two or three separate occasions Peter heard the Lord say that He must go to Jerusalem, suffer at the hands of the elders, the high priests and the scribes, and be killed—but that He would be raised from the dead after three days. Peter could not bear such a thought. He began to pity the Lord, and he told Him: "Be it far from thee, Lord [or, God have mercy on thee]: this shall never be unto thee." We might think that Jesus would probably comfort Peter by saying: "Your love for Me is indeed great, Peter, but I cannot avoid going to Jerusalem to die." The Lord instead rebuked His disciple in the strongest of terms: "Get thee behind me, Satan: thou art a stumbling-block unto me: for thou mindest not the things of God, but the things of men." The Lord made a distinctive choice here: He chose death.

If there be anyone in this world who has chosen the cross and walked the narrow way, I am sure that person must have tasted the abundance of God's grace and the sweetness of God's love. Recently the paper called *Intelligence* recorded the martyrdom of two lady missionaries in Fukien. They were both British and served in that province. Bandits had kidnapped them, and a month ago they were killed. They were both aged and very deep in the Lord. One of these missionaries had written a poem before being killed. She had entitled it "The Martyr," in which were found these words: "A martyr's face is the face of an angel! A martyr's heart is the heart of a lion!" The face of an angel is most beautiful and the heart of a lion is most majestic. How marvelous that a martyr should write a martyr's poem! Before she died, she had penned a letter to her friend, saying: "The grace of God is sufficient for me. Though environment tells me how dangerous and difficult a situation I am in, yet never in my life have I been so near to God."

Another China Inland Mission missionary was also kidnapped, though later released. A friend asked him about his experience. He answered that on the night when he heard the buzzing of the bullets and there seemed no way of coming out of it alive, he was filled with peace and joy which he had never experienced since his regeneration.

There must be a reason behind anyone being a martyr. There must be in that person a most unusual power. Never for a moment think that God pays us the lowest wages while demanding us "weaklings" to bear unbearable responsibility. No, our God gives us butter and honey so that we may be able to forsake all things, even to die for the truth. And this is neither a false nor an empty word being uttered here. I know it, and many others know it. All who are able to forsake things, to not seek anything for themselves but to choose the difficult part, have a tremendous power in them, even as Christ had. Because of the power in Him the Lord Jesus could refuse the evil and choose the good.

Five: At His Transfiguration (Luke 9.28–31)

On the Mount of Transfiguration the Lord manifested the peak of His humanity before God as well as before men. The Bible never teaches that we are without blemish in this life (we do indeed have faults and blemishes); it only maintains that God is able to keep us blameless in this life. But in this life our Lord is without any blemish at all. I have spoken before concerning the transfiguration of Jesus on the mountain. Many commentators agree that the Lord could well have ascended to heaven from that mount and God could not have refused receiving Him back into heaven. In this connection, take note of this passage: "The earth beareth fruit of herself; first the blade, then the ear, then the full grain in the ear. But when the fruit is ripe, straightway he putteth forth the sickle, because the harvest is come" (Mark 4.28,29). Since the Lord had ripened (that is to say, He had by this time become fully matured), He could have been received back. Yet He talked with Moses and Elijah about His departure which He was about to accomplish at Jerusalem. And when He returned to the valley below, Jesus was even more determined to go to Jerusalem: His face was unalterably set towards that objective. He chose death.

Here, then, we see another choice of our Lord. Jesus is able to refuse to ascend to heaven from the Mount of Transfiguration and to choose the way to Jerusalem and death because He had eaten the butter and the honey of heaven. He is able not to ascend to see His Father but to descend to the cross because He has tasted the grace as well as the love of God.

Without God's grace and God's love, who can endure such suffering? Some children may suffer for their parents, but they suffer unwillingly. Some parents may suffer for their children, yet not without murmuring at times. Some students may obey their teachers under compulsion. Only Christ is able to make the difficult though good choice with a willing heart because He has eaten butter and honey—the most abundant and the sweetest of things.

Six: Entering Jerusalem (John 12.12–28)

The two most glorious occasions in our Lord's lifetime are the Mount of Transfiguration experience and His entry into Jerusalem. When He entered Jerusalem, many people took branches of palm trees and went forth to meet Him. They cried out: "Hosanna: Blessed is he that cometh in the name of the Lord, even the King of Israel." These were words uttered by the Jews. At that time, the Lord still had many friends. Lazarus had recently been raised from the dead, some people had prepared a feast for Him, and certain Greeks came to Philip saying, We would see Jesus. Even His enemies, the Pharisees, said to one another: "Behold how ye prevail nothing; lo, the world is gone after him." At that juncture, He could have gotten anything He wanted. But when Andrew and Philip came to tell the Lord Jesus of the Greeks' desire to see Him, what did He reply? "Verily, verily, I say unto you, Except a grain of wheat fall into the earth and die, it abideth by itself alone; but if it die, it beareth much fruit." Here He made one more choice. He could gain glory and become King, but He chose otherwise. How my heart is deeply moved by what He said: "Except a grain of wheat fall into the earth and die, it abideth by itself alone; but if it die, it beareth much fruit."

"Now is my soul troubled; and what shall I say?"

This indicates how the Lord's heart and mouth consulted with each other. "Father, save me from this hour. But for this cause I came unto this hour." The Lord could have asked the Father to deliver Him from that hour, yet He knew He came for that very hour. Once again He refused the evil and chose the good. Formerly when we noticed these things, we wondered how He could make such choices. Now, though, the Bible in Isaiah tells us how it is that He can choose the good and refuse the evil: it is because He has tasted the butter and honey, the abundance of grace and the sweetness of love.

Seven: In Gethsemane (Matt. 26.36–46)

Finally in the Garden of Gethsemane, the Lord made the greatest choice! There He could say, I wish not to die: "My Father, if it be possible, let this cup pass away from me." But He instantly added: "Nevertheless, not as I will, but as thou wilt." Though He saw the dreadfulness of the cup, He dared not follow His own will. He was not afraid of the cup; it was only that His holy virtue rebelled against sin-bearing. Before He knew that the cup and the will of God had been joined into one, He could legitimately ask, "If it be possible, let this cup pass away from me"; but that was followed immediately by, "not as I will, but as thou wilt." Hence in the Garden of Gethsemane He chose the will of God and equally rejected what was not God's will. And what did Jesus finally say to Peter? "The cup which the Father hath given me, shall I not drink it?" (John 18.11)

Let me tell you that if there had been no Gethsemane, there could have been no cross. Without the obedience of the Garden there would not have been the death of Calvary. Obedience preceded the cross. Our Lord "humbled himself, becoming obedient even unto death, yea, the death of the cross" (Phil. 2.8). Many people flee from before the face of the cross because they have not done well in the consecration of Gethsemane. They do not have the power in them. But our Lord had butter and honey; therefore, He could choose the good and refuse the evil.

It requires great power to be obedient! If God does not fill your heart first, you will not succeed, no matter how you try externally. We need to learn to draw near to God daily and receive from heaven both butter and honey so that day by day we may live on earth choosing the good and refusing the evil.

I speak to you today in this manner because I have a deep sense within me that the return of the Lord is imminent and that the kingdom is at hand. Henceforth, temptations will be greater, dangers will be multiplied, and deceptions will be deepened. Previously it was the matter of getting rid of sin; now it is the matter of getting rid of pleasure. Formerly it was to receive the stripping of God; now it is to obey with a willing heart. Earlier it was a case of bearing the yoke reluctantly; now it is to choose the cross voluntarily.

We foresee today many things which will befall us hereafter if we do not know how to refuse the evil and choose the good. For Satan will offer us more advantages, the world will appear more gracious by giving us many things, and our environment will also be more helpful. If we do not refuse, we cannot overcome. How can we overcome the world? If the Lord had not chosen death, He could have lived because it was possible for Him not to have died. Oh do let us notice one thing: that no matter what is placed before us, we shall be able to choose with singleness of heart only because we have received the heavenly butter and honey. Hence we must daily receive butter and honey from heaven that we may know what to choose and what to refuse. Let us not allow our environment to choose for us.

4 | Spiritual Or Mental?

> Who also made us sufficient as ministers of a new covenant; not of the letter, but of the spirit: for the letter killeth, but the spirit giveth life. (2 Cor. 3.6)

The word "letter" here points to the law. By comparing the law with the Holy Spirit we find that the law can do nothing to man but kill him because it does not possess the power of giving life as does the Spirit. "It is the spirit," says Jesus, "that giveth life" (John 6.63). Nothing except the Holy Spirit can give life. Even the life of God is in the Holy Spirit. Moreover, our physical world was restored at the beginning through the brooding activity of the Holy Spirit (Gen. 1.2b mg.). And the birth of the Lord Jesus, He being God incarnated, came about by the overshadowing power of the Most High. According to the revelation of the Bible, whatever possesses life or gives life is in, or by virtue of, the Holy Spirit. But since the law is established in letter and not in the Holy Spirit, it causes man to die.

Yet not only in the *Old* Covenant is there the "letter" (that is, the law) which kills; even the *New* Covenant has its "letter." What the Old Covenant stresses is the law, yet the law — as the Scripture tells us — is of God, being holy and righteous and good (Rom. 7.12). But because the Holy Spirit is lacking in it, the law becomes the letter which kills, just as do the many other "letters" in the world. Yet we discover a similar possibility in the New Covenant. For although many truths, commandments, exhortations and teachings in the gospel of the New Covenant are of God and can regulate human conduct and influence men's moral behavior, nevertheless, if they are divorced from the power of the Holy Spirit they too will be transformed into the letter that kills.

Without God's Spirit, All Is Dead and Powerless

This truth just enunciated above is unfortunately overlooked by many believers: that outside the Holy Spirit there is no life, that outside of God's Spirit all is dead. We must see clearly that aside from wholly relying on the operation of the Spirit of God, we are absolutely useless. Though we acknowledge the corruption of the flesh, we too often do not understand the power of the Holy Spirit. And hence, in spite of our confession, we are not delivered from the domain of the flesh. God will lead us to the place where we will live entirely by His Spirit. He wants us to realize that all our works and deeds and prayers and seeking for truth are dead enterprises if they are not the result of the working of the Holy Spirit in us and are not produced by His power. In God's eyes these are dead works destined for the tomb.

The call of God today is for His children to obtain the more abundant life. He wants us to be rid of death, to overcome death. Yet how our attention is so often set on overcoming sins but not in overcoming death. Even so, God will deliver us not only from the law of sin but also from the law of death: "for the law of the Spirit of life in Christ Jesus made me free from the law of sin and of death" (Rom. 8.2). The Holy Spirit alone can give this life. Where He is lacking, there is no life but there is instead the filling up of death. Christians should not only refrain from sinning, they should also overcome death and be filled with life. God hates death as much as He hates sin. Sin separates us from Him; and death hinders us from communion with Him. To overcome sin is negative, to be filled with life is positive.

We need to see that whoever is in Christ is alive. How is he alive? By the Holy Spirit, for "the law of the Spirit of life in Christ Jesus . . ."

Hence what our verse from 2 Corinthians 3.6 reveals is this: (1) that whatever is of the flesh is dead, but (2) that even in the perfect law given by God, if it is outside the Holy Spirit, it too is dead. For the letter kills.

The Word of God and the Spirit of God

The word of God and the Spirit of God are inseparable. God gives His word to us by giving us the Bible, but at the same time He adds a condition: men must receive His word in the power of His Spirit. God backs up His word by His Spirit; He proves His word with His Spirit. He uses His Spirit to preserve His word so that no one will fall short. Whoever contacts God's word without contacting the Holy Spirit will not see the power of God's word. For without the Spirit of God the word of God becomes dead letter.

"Now the natural man receiveth not the things of the Spirit of God: for they are foolishness unto him" (1 Cor. 2.14a). To an unbeliever who searches the Scriptures by his own wisdom the Bible is as good as dead. This does not imply that the Bible is not the word of God, nor that God's word has no power. It simply means that without the Holy Spirit the Bible in the experience of that unbeliever is merely a dead and powerless book.

The word of God remains the same. For some people, however, it becomes life, whereas for others it is only letter. What is the reason for such a difference? None other than because the first class of persons receives the word of God in the power of the Holy Spirit while the second class tries to understand the same word in the wisdom of their mind.

The word of God is powerful and has life. Yet when a person receives it solely with the mind, he will not experience the power and life of God's word. Whatever truth is accepted simply with the mind becomes a mere thought for that person. Such truth has no effectiveness in his walk. He cannot depend upon it in time of need. Though he may know the argument, the fact or the procedure, he will not be able to obtain the power therein. For him in his life, the truth is not truth but only empty teaching, because he cannot demonstrate its truthfulness.

For a believer to know whether he has received the word of God in the power of the Holy Spirit, he need only ask if he finds the word powerful in his life when he receives it; because God sends the Holy Spirit to prove to the believer the truthfulness of His word. Consequently, if the word of God fails to be proven, it is due to the fact that the power of the Spirit is lacking in it.

The danger today is that believers hear God's word, read the Bible or seek the truth with only the wisdom of the mind. God joins His word and His Spirit together, but men will either separate His word from His Spirit or His Spirit from His word. The peril of these two extremes is equally as great in either direction. For in separating the word of God from the Spirit of God, what the person obtains will be mere idea or an ideal. And in separating the Spirit of God from the word of God, what that person becomes will be an oddity. More people fall into the trap of the first extreme than into the trap of the second.

Many people read the Bible as though perusing a scientific book. It is as if, with a good mind, some good instruction and good effort, they can understand the Bible. Such kind of research may enable a person to know something of Biblical history and doctrine, but it will not help him to experience the power of God's word. We must be brought by the Lord to the place where we will depend on His Spirit in the reading of His word. We will then understand His truth in His power. The Holy Spirit alone is able to apply the word of God with its life and power to a believer's walk. Accepting the truth merely in the power of the mind will not enable him to realize this life and power in his daily experience.

A Real Difference

What is the real difference between receiving the truth in the power of the Spirit and receiving it in the power of the mind?

(A) If a person receives some religious truth from a book or from a teacher or even from the Bible itself without the need of prayer, of laying down one's power or of depending completely on the Holy Spirit, he is receiving that truth in the power of his mind. For the acceptance of truth in the power of the mind means receiving it directly from a book, teacher or the Bible while by-passing the Holy Spirit. The Pharisees knew the Scriptures directly in this way; hence what they ended up possessing was something dead, void of any living experience before God—for the word of God leads people to draw nigh to Him, and God himself is Spirit. But reading God's word without His Spirit fails to effect any contact between a man and God.

(B) The Galatian believers lapsed into keeping the law after they had first believed in the gospel and had begun walking by faith. So Paul asked them: "Received ye the Spirit by the works of the law, or by the hearing of faith?" (Gal. 3.2) What the apostle meant was that they had indeed begun with faith but now trusted in works. He further asked them: "Having begun in the Spirit, are ye now perfected in the flesh?" (3.3) What he indicated was that they had indeed begun by depending on the Holy Spirit but now they had commenced depending on the flesh. Through these two questions we discover a most important principle: that whatever is of the Holy Spirit is by faith and whatever is of the flesh is by works. The Spirit and faith are joined in one just as the flesh and works are joined in one.

Hence seeking the truth in the power of the mind and seeking the truth in the power of the Spirit has one vital difference between them—which is, that the first is without faith while the second requires it.

In order to receive the truth in the Holy Spirit one must have faith. To receive in the power of the mind merely gives one some understanding, but to receive in the Holy Spirit gives one faith. Let us illustrate this. The believer's co-death with Christ is the source of a Christian's life and power. This is a truth we have put much emphasis on and one we frequently preached about. Today quite a few believers have already understood this truth, and they have even risen up to testify to it. But how many of them have actually received this truth *in the Holy Spirit*? Their speech betrays the inadequacy of their experience. I know a certain brother, for example, who considers himself as really knowing the truth of co-death. Once he was preaching and said this: You should die; if at times you cannot die, put yourself to death in the power of the cross. Now these words sound very spiritual, but actually they are rather superficial. Why? Because he has no faith, but still hopes to work it out himself. This shows that concerning the truth of co-death he only understands it in his mind but lacks the power in the Holy Spirit.

How can we explain it? If a person wants to actually experience the power of the Holy Spirit he must first have faith, for the Holy Spirit will work only because man has believed in God's word. Faith comes first, and then the working of the Spirit in man follows. Without faith the truth which one knows is but an idea, for the Holy Spirit has not worked into him what the truth has accomplished.

Let us return to the truth of co-death for a moment. The Holy Spirit teaches us that when Christ died, He had already included us in His death. And just as Christ having died for us is a fact, so we having died with Christ is also a fact. Just as the death of Christ is real, so our death is as real too. Even as we are delivered from the penalty of sin by believing in the death of Christ, so likewise we are delivered from the power of sin by believing that we ourselves have *already* died with Christ. This is the way God's word teaches us. Thus it comes down to whether we believe or do not believe. If we believe, the Holy Spirit will bear witness to God's word and cause us to experience the reality that "sin shall not have dominion over" us (Rom. 6.14). And at this point we may truly say that we have received the truth in the power of the Spirit.

Hence we can now discern the order required for

receiving any truth in the Holy Spirit: (1) the teaching of the Bible, (2) the faith of the believer, and (3) the working of the Holy Spirit. None of these three factors can be missing. But the one who receives a truth with his mind does not have faith. By his searching the Scriptures or by his listening to others' teaching he may come to *understand* the argument of co-death and he may *know* that one who is dead is freed from sin. Nevertheless, in all this he lacks faith; and hence he cannot see clearly the position of the old man in the death of Christ nor can he say he is a person *already* crucified with Christ. So that in his own experience he is continually attempting to put himself to death, and when he advises other people on this matter he cannot help but say: you ought to die (even as the "certain brother" in the earlier illustration advised in his preaching). Even if at times he offers up some prayers and begins to understand the reality of his co-death with Christ which causes him to confess with his mouth that he is a crucified person, he nonetheless in his daily living trusts more in self-crucifixion than in believing in his having already been crucified on the cross with Christ.

(C) If truth is accepted in the Holy Spirit, it will invariably become the experience of that person. The Spirit does not reveal a truth merely to give the believer some more mental material. He preeminently desires to lead him into what the truth says. Mental comprehension may cause a person to praise the truth, but it will not give him the help of the truth. Many people may approve of a certain truth, they may even love such a truth; nevertheless, they only have it in their mind. If a truth has no effectual power in a person's life, by this we ought to know that that truth is only in his mind and does not carry with it the power of God's Spirit.

We need to see the difference as well as the relationship between principle and practice. A principle must be obtained through the revelation of God's Spirit. Due to the much accumulation of knowledge and to the multitude of teachers, many have come to understand numerous principles on the spiritual life. Yet so often these are solely in their mind. To put these principles into practice in life they need the divine Spirit. The mind is capable of understanding principles, but the Spirit of God alone can put these principles into practice. In working on an algebra problem it is easy for a student to solve an equation; it is somewhat difficult, though, to put a subject into the equation. Similarly, it is fairly easy to learn a spiritual principle with the mind, but to put this principle to practice in life is beyond the ability of the mind. He who studies geography may know the capitals and the big cities of the world's nations, along with their respective agricultural, industrial and commercial situations, without perhaps so much as even having to step out of his house. By doing research through brain power, therefore, a person can understand a great deal of the Bible. Without depending on the Holy Spirit, however, he will have no experience at all.

Today's danger is that many people are seeking the knowledge of the Bible with their mind. They understand a few mysteries, comprehend many spiritual principles, dig out some deeper meanings of God's word, and even appreciate to a certain degree the accomplished work of Christ. Yet these are all in their mind. These are not given them by the Holy Spirit and there is therefore no practical power involved. With the result that the Bible is reduced to the level of a scientific treatise in which the reader and the writer have no personal contact whatsoever. On the other hand, the word of God—though its contents had been spoken long ago and later recorded in what we have as the Bible—is nonetheless in the Holy Spirit even as God is in the Spirit. If the reader receives God's word directly without leaning on the power of the Spirit, he will have no relationship with God. This will reduce the value of God's word and make it as one of the dead books of the world.

Understanding of the Scriptures may help to clarify man's thought and concepts, but it will have no practical effectiveness in his spiritual experience and work. This may explain in part why the truth may indeed be preached and yet it has no power on the speaker as well as on the hearers. If the truth is entirely circumscribed within the mind of the speaker, it will only reach the mind of the hearers.

Having the truth without having the Spirit of the truth is almost totally useless. When the Lord Jesus told His disciples that He is the truth, He proceeded to tell them that the Spirit of truth would come to lead them into all truths. Let us realize here and now that the believer is joined to the truth through the Spirit of truth; otherwise, truth remains as truth and the believer remains as believer. Just as the disciples of old could not really understand and experience Christ before they received God's Spirit, so believers today are not able to genuinely know and experience the word of God except by the power of the Holy Spirit.

Real Spiritual Work

Who can tell how much of the preaching today is but from the wisdom of man? The preaching may be quite profound and include genuine spiritual lessons; even the faith displayed in it may be sound and the interpretations presented be logical; further, such preaching may at the same time touch the hearers by affecting their conduct and morals to a certain extent. Nevertheless, such preaching may not be of the Holy Spirit but of man's wisdom. We should even be open to the possibility that the maxims spoken by the deeply experienced, though actually producing some seemingly satisfactory consequences by stirring up and changing people, may not in fact be the result of the working of the Holy Spirit.

Man's flesh must be eliminated, man's efforts must be reduced to nothing, the old man with its wisdom and ability must be concluded at the cross. Since God possesses everything and is able to do everything, He must be all. Everything must be done in the power of the Holy Spirit. Some people may think that if man is reduced to zero the word of God will greatly suffer — that everything will cease its progress and fruit will be diminished if not eradicated altogether. But what we stress is real spiritual work and real spiritual fruit before God. Only under such circumstances as these will there be the greatest spiritual usefulness. The work done in the wisdom of man may be prosperous in many ways, but it lacks true spiritual value and is of little use in God's hand. The Holy Spirit alone can do the work of God. The less the place of man, the more manifest will be the power of the Spirit. The work of the Spirit in only five minutes has more spiritual usefulness than all our labor through the night that gets nothing. Is it not far better to wait for the Lord's command and obtain a netful of fish in but one casting?

The Place of Brain Power

Such being the case, is brain power totally useless in the truth of God? No, the brain (or the mind) has its place. We ought to distinguish the use of man's spirit and his head. He who reveals the truth is the Holy Spirit, and that which receives the revelation of the Holy Spirit is the renewed spirit of man. The renewed spirit of man alone can receive revelation, the brain cannot be the organ for receiving it.

Let us see that the work of the mind is to transmit. A renewed mind helps to transmit to other people the truth received in revelation. But the renewed mind itself does not discover the truth of God. An old mind may hinder a person in the work of transmission, but if his spirit is already renewed, he can still receive revelation. God sets aside the old creation. Natural *deficiency* will not hinder people from receiving revelation, yet neither will natural *efficiency* help people to receive revelation. An excellent mind may aid in transmitting, but it cannot give revelation to himself or to others.

The Vanity of Natural Talent

Due to their surpassing natural ability, many teachers of God's word are able to search out, understand, and deliver some truths to other people. And many there are who say they are being helped by such teachers. However, speaking frankly, these teachers have not accomplished anything of real spiritual worth. People with more natural talents usually become teachers of the less talented, but their spiritual state is exactly the same or else, in some cases, the taught are even more spiritual than the teachers.

The most perilous situation in the church today lies in the fact that many of the famous in high places are there not because they are actually more spiritual but because they have higher natural talents. We refer not only to the learned and the wise in the secular world, but especially to the famous in the spiritual world. Many Bible teachers and congregational leaders nowadays are successful not because they know more of the Holy Spirit than do other people but because they turn their superior natural talents to the Bible and spiritual things. How many of the so-called spiritual ones are in fact not spiritual! And why? because the Holy Spirit is not in them! The contents of their teaching or preaching are simply the spiritual thoughts *of the mind*. Much teaching and preaching is but the result of research and not the learning of lessons from the Holy Spirit. Naturally, therefore, such leaders can only help the minds of other people.

How many Christians have the idea that as long as natural talent is used in the proper place it can do the work of glorifying God! Yet natural talent is *natural* talent; even if it is engaged in *spiritual* things, such talent is not acceptable to God. The Holy Spirit may use natural talent, but such must be completely surrendered to Him. God needs individuals who are full of the Holy Spirit more than He needs any other kind of person. We ought to be very clear on the important point raised by the following question: Is it because our thoughts are more clever that we are to lead other people, or is it because we actually know the Spirit of God?

Must Have the Holy Spirit

God wishes us to know deeply that just as the Scriptures are *inspired* by the Holy Spirit, so the Scriptures require the revelation of the Holy Spirit. Just as the Bible was written by men moved by God's Spirit, so the Bible also needs His Spirit to move people in their reading of it. Just as the Sacred Book was recorded by the Holy Spirit, so the Book also needs the enlightment of the Holy Spirit. Here the wisdom of men is useless. God would have us also know that even the clearest interpretation of the Bible is not adequate. Our power must come from the Holy Spirit. Man's wisdom may cause people to understand the meaning of the Scriptures, out it will not give them the benefit of the truth.

In seeking the truth, many come with the wrong motive. If they are not seeking to satisfy their own lust for knowing, they are preparing messages to teach others. Their basic motive is to solve mental difficulties and not to cultivate their own spiritual life. Since such is their intention, they feel quite comforted if they are able, in the end, to understand. For they can now teach others. Clearly, they are not seeking for spiritual reality.

Only after we have realized that man can only be saved by the Holy Spirit, that truth can only be apprehended in the Holy Spirit, that prayer can only be heard through the Holy Spirit, and that our spiritual life can only be advanced in the Holy Spirit, will we truly believe and depend on the Holy Spirit. How frequently do we actually ask God for light? Perhaps few really pray for light. Probably we spend more time in thinking, searching and seeking than in praying. This is why the spiritual walk of countless believers is cut and dried though they understand many truths.

In much modern preaching, more emphasis is placed on mental content than on having life in the spirit. We should know that works of real value are done in people's spirit and not in their mind. The work which God acknowledges is solely of one kind: the work of His Spirit in the spirit of man in pouring into man's spirit the life of Christ — whether it be giving life for the first time or for giving it more abundantly. Merely receiving the rational approval of men without there being the pouring in of the life of Christ into men is a work of vanity.

God's Discipline

Such a lesson is most difficult to learn. When man's flesh rebels against God, it loves to sin and is unwilling to obey the law of God. Even when it tries to please God, the flesh proclaims its independence of Him as though it can serve Him without waiting for divinely given power. Hence it will never depend on God's Spirit. While it seeks the truth, man's mental flesh tends to think its own wisdom to be already sufficient. God is therefore compelled to let His children go through painful experiences in order to teach them that whatever is obtained by their own power with their own wisdom can neither help themselves nor others, and thus they may be willing to forsake all their fleshly strength and wisdom and seek for the Holy Spirit and His power. For instance, many works seem to have a promising beginning but soon lose their earlier enthusiastic support and gradually die out so as to alert God's workers that something must have gone wrong. The excitement of the flesh lasts only for a moment. Thus God is leading his servants to see how empty and vain are their works that they may begin anew with the Holy Spirit. How painful must such experience be!

Or take as another example of God's discipline the following situation. There are many believers who regard themselves as knowing a great deal. They think they can be more than conquerors by knowing many truths. Yet they are defeated again and again in their lives. Though they try with every effort to grasp these truths, they still find themselves helpless. For in the time of battle, the truths they know so well turn out to be like weapons of straw. They weep and shed many tears. Can the truths of God be wrong, or is there something else wrong? Oh, God wants them to see that the Holy Spirit alone can wield the Sword of the Spirit (which is the word and truth of God). For the flesh to use the Sword of the Spirit is like David trying to wear Saul's armor that was totally unfit for battling Goliath. Although they may well know the truth in their head, these people have not depended on the Holy Spirit to make such their life.

The Process for Receiving Truth

The truth of God usually comes upon a believer in two successive steps: (1) in the mind, and (2) in the spirit. Frequently it comes to the spirit later than to the mind. The gap of time may be several months or even several years. After God gives a certain truth to a believer (that is to say, after the believer begins to know this truth in his mind), He will work in the environment so as to bring the believer into a place where he cannot overcome except by this truth. Then and there the believer will know the truth in the power of the Holy Spirit and have satisfying experience of it. How sad, though, that as soon as a believer knows in his mind God's truth, he is so contented with this that he either will not seek for an experience of it or will commence to teach other people concerning it. And thus it is hard for God to bring him to the reality of the truth.

With Or without Power Is the Unmistakable Sign

In the past we have often stressed that the Holy Spirit is full of life and power; and hence, whatever is of God's Spirit will without fail have life and power in it. So that when we see a person who knows a certain truth and yet the truth does not help his spiritual life nor give him power since it merely fills his mind with a beautiful thought but does not succor him in time of fierce temptation, we doubt whether there is in him the work of God's Spirit. Let us not be satisfied with merely meaningful words. We must seek the power of God. How many times people talk about the truth of the Holy Spirit without their having even a little of His power. What a believer lacks is none other than more of the life of God.

It is most interesting to notice that if a person understands the truth of God with his mind, he must frequently be exercised to grasp this truth. But if he knows the truth in the power of the Holy Spirit and maintains it in the same power as well, he will not need to grasp the truth in time of need as though like a drowning person grasping hold of a rope; rather, he himself will be grasped and saved by the truth through the Holy Spirit. This distinction is most evident.

Let us realize that the truth of God apart from the

Spirit of God is dead. Just as the life of a man cannot afford to be momentarily interrupted, even so, the power given by the Spirit must always be renewed and supplied. What the Spirit of God does at one time may not be the same thing He will do every time. Each contact with Him brings in fresh power. Our communication with the Holy Spirit is not once and for all. For this reason, in the receiving of God's truth we must continually depend on God's power. When, for example, we hear of other people's spiritual experience, we naturally will try to imitate. We expect God to lead us in the same way and grant us the same result. How often we are disappointed in this respect. Yet it is because their experience is of the Holy Spirit while ours is purely of the mind. God has to allow us to be frequently disappointed so that we will seek Him by *directly* depending on the Holy Spirit. Copying with the mind is absolutely futile. And this same conclusion can be applied to our quoting the Scriptures to gain spiritual power. We assume because the Bible was inspired by the Holy Spirit that there must be power in quoting more of its words. To our surprise, though, the result is negative. And why? because the Holy Spirit must *speak again and afresh*.

What we must therefore seek today is for the Holy Spirit to give us life through the truth. We must seek for His revelation and His application. We must let Him transfer the truth from our head to our heart. May we believe in the word of God with all our heart, reckoning whatever He says to be true. May we never be content with the knowledge of mere theory.

5 | **The Dividing of Soul and Spirit**

The word of God is living, and active, and sharper than any two-edged sword, and piercing even to the dividing of soul and spirit, of both joints and marrow, and quick to discern the thoughts and intents of the heart. And there is no creature that is not manifest in his sight: but all things are naked and laid open before the eyes of him with whom we have to do. (Heb. 4.12,13)

One

The dividing of soul and spirit is exceedingly essential since it concerns the Christian's spiritual growth. How can a Christian seek for that which is spiritual if he does not even know the distinction between spirit and soul? He will often mistake the soulish for the spiritual, and thus stay long in the realm of soulish living instead of seeking for the spiritual. The word of God cites many times the features of the spirit as well as those of the soul. For instance, the Bible records being sorrowful in the spirit as well as being sorrowful in the soul, it mentions being joyful in the spirit as much as being joyful in the soul. Hence people draw the conclusion that since the expressions of the spirit and the soul are the same, the spirit must be the soul. This is like saying, "Because you eat food and I too eat food, therefore you must be me." Yet Hebrews 4.12 says that "the word of God is living, and active, and sharper than any two-edged sword, and piercing even to the *dividing* of soul and spirit." Since soul and spirit may be separated, soul must be soul and spirit must be spirit.

We are shown in Genesis 2 that when God first created man He "formed man of the dust of the ground, and breathed into his nostrils the breath of life; and man became a living soul" (v.7) This breath of life is man's spirit since it came directly from God. As it touched man's body, the soul was produced— and man became a living soul. Man's spirit has God-consciousness, knows God's voice, and is able to communicate with Him. But after the fall of Adam, his spirit became dead to God. Thereafter the spirit of Adam (and of all his descendants) was so oppressed by the soul that his spirit was knit intimately with the soul. When a person is saved, though, his spirit becomes alive to God; but due to the close uniting of the spirit with the soul for such a long period, it requires the word of God to divide or separate them.

Two

Though the expressions of the soul and the spirit

appear similar, they belong to different realms—they come from two different sources. When you are joyful today, this joy may come from the soul or from the spirit. Joy is being expressed, but there is a difference from where it comes. Likewise, you may feel sorrowful today. Now sorrow is sorrow; yet it may come from different sources. From whence does it come? This is the question God will himself ask. Does it come out from your soul or out from your spirit?

For example, God promised Abraham he could have a son. At that time Abraham was already advanced in age and seemingly without much hope. After having waited for a long while with God's promise still unfulfilled, his wife came up with a plan to let him marry her maid Hagar, and thus Abraham obtained Ishmael. But after fourteen years, God caused Abraham's wife Sarah to give birth to Isaac. As we read through Genesis chapters 15, 16, 17 and 21, we may not perceive what Isaac and Ishmael represent; but wait until we read Galatians 4 in the New Testament and we discern immediately the meaning of both. Paul tells us that the one (Isaac) is born through promise but the other (Ishmael) is born after the flesh (v.23). Do you now see the difference? People reason that as long as they obtain a son, all is well. But God will inquire as to how that son is born. We want a son, be he Isaac or Ishmael. Yet the word of God says that Ishmael represents what is fleshly while Isaac represents what is spiritual. What Ishmael stands for is that which man obtains in his own wisdom and by his own power; what Isaac stands for is that which is out from God and given by God.

What therefore is soulish? Soulish is that which is done by oneself. And what therefore is spiritual? It is that which is done by God. And these two are radically different. A person can do something without any need for waiting upon God and trusting in Him. Such action is fleshly and it is soulish. But if a person cannot speak before God speaks, cannot move except God moves first; if he must look to God, wait and depend on Him—then that person and that action is spiritual. Let us thus ask ourselves if all we do is in the Holy Spirit? This is such an important question. Frequently there is nothing wrong in what we do, nevertheless there is condemnation registered within us when we do it. The reason for this inward sense is not that what we do outwardly is necessarily wrong but because the thing we do is not initiated from God— that is to say, it is not the outcome of the working of the Holy Spirit in us.

Three

I Corinthians 3 talks about building. It refers to our work and service for God. Some build with gold, silver and precious stones, whereas others build with wood, hay and stubble. What is the work done with gold, silver and precious stones? What is the work done with wood, hay and stubble? In the Scriptures the gold, silver and precious stones point to what is of God: gold represents the glory which comes from the Father; silver, the redemption which is the work of the Son; and precious stones, the work of the Holy Spirit, since these stones are compounds formed underground through intense heat. That which has about it the eternal glory of God, the cross of the Son, and the organization of the Holy Spirit is called gold, silver and precious stones. To what, then, do the wood, hay and stubble point? Obviously, all which comes out of man himself: the glory of man is like straw (hay) and flowers; the nature of man is like wood, and the work of man is like stubble.

Now gold, silver and precious stones do not appear on the surface of the earth. They have to be dug up from the deep recesses of the earth. Wood, hay and stubble, on the other hand, grow on the face of the earth and are easily obtainable. Hence whatever comes out of the depths as a result of what takes place deep within shows the work of God in them; but whatever can be done by the flesh from out of man has no value whatsoever. What can be easily done does not possess much spiritual value, for this is merely outward; but what comes from the depths because it is from God is worth much.

This difference is noticeable in preaching. Some in preaching need to wait upon God until a burden is formed, just as in conception. This is the work of gold, silver and precious stones. Some preach because their brain is sharp and their lips are eloquent. They can also remember many things. Therefore they can stand up and preach. They actively work, but all this is wood, hay and stubble in the sight of God—hence having so little spiritual value.

Once a brother was preaching at a certain place. From the human standpoint, the outward conditions were excellent. He should therefore have been reasonably happy. Yet strangely enough, as time went on he found himself deflated within. Though he worked vigorously, within himself he felt hungrier, drier and increasingly deflated. Once the work was done he had to confess his sins before God and to acknowledge that it was done by himself.

The question here does not turn upon the outward condition of the work but upon the matter of who primarily is doing the work; that is to say, where does it originate? For instance, one preacher may learn to say the same words and preach the same message as another, yet people feel he is just a clever person; whereas all sense the other is a man who knows God. With some servants of the Lord we bow our heads, saying, "God is here"; with others, we can only say he is clever and eloquent. If you touch God, you can cause other people to touch Him too; but if you touch only the soul, you only cause people to touch you yourself. How vast is the difference!

Four

This is not only true in the matter of seeing God but is equally true in our personal life on earth. One day a Christian went to talk with a servant of God. Being somewhat fearful of criticism, this Christian exerted his utmost strength to keep himself humble during the conversation. His attitude as well as his word were quite humble in tone. But while he was trying to be humble, those who sat nearby detected the strain of it. Now if a person is truly humble, he has no need to exercise so much effort. Actually, this Christian was simulating humility, and therefore it required great effort indeed. Can you say he was not humble? Well, he appeared to be so, but in point of fact it was man-made humility, and such belongs to the soul. For if God had worked in this brother, he could have been humble quite naturally. He himself would not have felt he was being humble, and those around him could have instead seen the work of God in him.

The lady who powders herself needs to look at the mirror frequently, but Moses' face shone often without his even being conscious of it. Whoever manifests the effects of God's working in him, that can be called spiritual. But the one who attempts to manufacture something must employ much strength; therefore he feels weary at being a Christian, although a Christian should never exercise his own strength in any case. We often judge that so long as a thing looks good it is probably all right, but God looks at the source as to whether it is of Him or an imitating in the power of the flesh.

The same could be said in another situation. Let us say that someone tries to be patient. Yet the more he tries to be patient, the more you with a discerning spirit feel sorry for him. But another person can be patient without his even being conscious of it. In that case you bow your head in thanks, saying that God has truly worked in that life. You notice that the second is of God but the first is out from himself. The difference lies not in respect of outward appearance but in respect of the source.

Oh do let us see that even though something out

of the natural life may appear quite spontaneously, that in itself does not signify that it is of the spirit. Someone, for example, is born with a gentle nature. Yet one day he will realize the total difference between his natural gentleness and Christ-given gentleness. Another individual may have been born with the natural capacity of loving people, yet he too will one day see the vast difference between his natural love and that love which comes from the Lord. The same will be true of the man who is born with natural humility in his character, but he also will one day discern the difference between God-given humility and his natural humility. This something which a person is born with tends to more easily substitute itself for what is spiritual than that which may be simulated by man. How often people will take what is naturally endowed in them as a substitute for what the Lord seeks to do in them. Yet as a matter of fact, what comes from the soul has no connection with God, since only what comes from the spirit is related to Him.

The meekest of all men will discover someday that temptation is stronger than his natural meekness. One day his meekness will be exhausted, his patience will come to an end: he can endure only so much, he can be meek only to a certain degree. Whereas the natural· strength of man is limited, the strength given us by the Lord is something totally different. What the Lord can do, I cannot do; for it is not I who do it but it is because the Lord being in me, I can therefore do it spontaneously. And afterwards I will marvel as to how such a thing could ever be. I can only bow my head and say, "I have no patience; yet, Lord, You are doing it in me." And without a doubt this that comes forth is truly something spiritual.

Five

We ought to acknowledge, however, that it is not easy for us ourselves to differentiate between what is spiritual and what is soulish merely by their outward appearances. It is futile to ask ourselves daily whether this is spiritual or that is soulish. Such questioning will have no spiritual value at all. We may ask, but we will not get an answer. We may analyze but we will not get any results. If we do not ask, we will certainly never know; yet even if we do ask, we still will not know.

In spiritual things, self-analysis will not only fail to show us the reality, it will even create spiritual paralysis. Real seeing and understanding comes only from God's illumination. As light shines, we just naturally see. We therefore do not need to ask ourselves questions; all we need to do is to ask God to cause His word to shine in us, for the word of God is living and most effective; it is sharper than any two-edged sword and pierces even to dividing between soul and spirit, between both joints and marrow. As soon as the word of God enters, you can immediately perceive what is soulish from what is spiritual. There is a judgment within you which is sharper than any human judgment. If you make a move, your inward sense tells you that this move is not right or not deep enough, or that it is you who are doing things and you who are trying to influence people. When you see inwardly, you really see. May God have mercy upon us by granting the inner light by which we may distinguish inwardly.

The dividing of soul and spirit is the foundation for a Christian to have discerning power. Yet whether we have this discerning power or not depends on inward illumination and not on outward instruction. What we should expect before God is that the entry of His word will give light so that He may show us what in our personal life and work is soulish or what is spiritual.

6 | Knowing the Self

> Thou shalt remember all the way which Jehovah thy
> God hath led thee these forty years in the wilderness,
> that he might humble thee, to prove thee, to know what
> was in thy heart, whether thou wouldest keep his com-
> mandments, or not. (Deut. 8.2)

To understand the reason for this verse we must
recall what God promised the children of Israel at
Mount Sinai. When he appeared on the Mount, God
said: "Now therefore, if ye will obey my voice indeed,
and keep my covenant, then ye shall be mine own
possession from among all peoples" (Ex. 19.5). When
the children of Israel heard this word, the people answered in one accord and without any hesitation: "All
that Jehovah hath spoken, we will do" (v.8). They
thought that since God had delivered them in such a
marvelous way and had led, supplied and protected

them, He would indeed be obeyed in whatever He might require of them.

However, what you say and promise may not be what your hands and feet will do. God will prove you on practical issues to determine if you really do worship Him and follow His will. Though you may think and even feel that you are perfectly willing to listen to God's word, the flesh has become so corrupted that what you might think and feel are not very trustworthy. That is why God must prove you as to your obedience of His commandments. And that is why Moses is telling the Israelites here that God had proved them "to know what was in thy heart, whether thou wouldest keep his commandments, or not." It was as though their promise being inadequate, they must be humbled and proved in the wilderness for forty years. Yet such "humbling" and "proving" were not designed for their spiritual downfall but for the manifestation of their real condition.

Without the humbling and proving experience of the wilderness and the subsequent defeats and rebellions, who would have known how utterly corrupt in their hearts these children of Israel were? Judging by their enthusiastic promise at the foot of Mount Sinai, we would think them to be a most obedient people. But they who promised so readily at Mount Sinai were the very people who later in the wilderness worshipped the golden calf, murmured against God and Moses, lusted to return to Egypt, and finally refused to enter Canaan. Nevertheless, after so many failures they at last realized that they were corrupt, that their flesh had absolutely nothing to be proud of, and that their self-importance in their thinking themselves better than other races was totally false since in point of fact they were not at all superior to any other nation in the world. Only then did they acknowledge that God had chosen them not because they were better than others but because of His free grace; for God had said to Moses, "I will have mercy on whom I have mercy, and I will have compassion on whom I have compassion. So then it is not of him that willeth, nor of him that runneth, but of God that hath mercy" (Rom. 9.15,16).

Now just as God had led the children of Israel in the Old Covenant period, so He seeks to lead His people today. What lesson He wants to teach His children now is the same lesson He tried to teach the Israelites before. And the lesson is *that we may know ourselves.* God desires His people to know that they are corrupt beyond repair, that they are full of sins, uncleannesses and weaknesses. He would lead the believers to the end of themselves. He would convince them to reckon their own selves as totally hopeless and absolutely useless so that they might cast themselves upon God in their helplessness and seek to know His will, depend on His power and accomplish His purpose.

Yet few believers are aware of this. Few really know they are full of corruption and uncleanness as well as know they are totally useless. Few deem themselves as having nothing. Most believers think of themselves as being trustworthy in many respects. And they feel they are stronger than other believers. Who, then, really knows himself through and through?

Let us understand that God has no need for our defeats and failures—only we do; for He knows full well how our flesh is corrupt and whether we stand and overcome or we fall and are defeated. He already knows our frame too well! He does not look for our flesh to achieve His righteousness for He realizes that except for sinning we can do nothing else. When we are doing good, He knows we are corrupt. And when we are doing evil, He again knows we are corrupt. He does not need to wait until we fall to realize our wretchedness. But it is *we* who need these defeats and falls, for *without* them *we are not able to know ourselves.* For while we experience smooth sailing, being often victorious and full of joy, we may regard ourselves as being fairly good and having possession of something that other people do not have. Though we may not dare to boast openly of anything, nevertheless, when we make some progress in spiritual life or have some success in spiritual work we cannot help but conceive the thought that now we are truly holy and powerful and excelling quite well. In such a state as this, it is easy to become careless and to lose the attitude of depending on God. Accordingly, the Lord permits us to fall from glory to dust. He allows us to sin, to fall, and to draw back. All these will cause us to know how utterly corrupted beyond natural help we are. We learn we are no different from the world's greatest and worst sinners. With the result that we dare not be self-reliant, self-glorifying and self-boasting anymore but will in all things cast ourselves upon God with fear and trembling. How we therefore need both defeat and failure to humble us, to cause us to know ourselves and the utter corruption of our flesh.

We recall how before we were saved and born again the Holy Spirit convicted us that we were sinners and that all our past goodness was as "a polluted garment" (Is. 64.6) which could neither cover our nakedness nor save us. We also became aware that even if we should try our best to do good thereafter, our own righteousness could never satisfy the demands of the law. We came to realize that we could never establish our own righteousness outside of Christ (Rom. 10.3). We therefore came to God in utter helplessness, accepted the Lord Jesus as our righteousness, and were saved through His redemption. Such was our past experience.

Yet how forgetful we are! At the time we were saved and born again, we knew we could not depend on our own good but must depend entirely on the work of Christ. The Holy Spirit showed us our terrible state of perdition, causing us to see that we were full of uncleanness and corruption and to perceive the total undependability of our own righteousness. Immediately following our salvation, and though we were full of joy because of the grace of forgiveness we had received, we remained humble. But after a while, we began to forget the first principle of salvation. Due to the new desire of the new life, we once again tried to meet the outside requirements with a righteousness of our own. We somehow lapsed into ignorance of the fact that when God told us at the time we were saved that our righteousness was absolutely useless He meant it was *eternally* useless. And just as He declared at the moment of our salvation how He would never be pleased with whatever came from ourselves—irrespective of their outward appearance—so He would declare the same thing to us ever afterwards.

We ought never forget that the way we obtained divine life is to be the same way that we are to nourish that life. The principle we learned at salvation must be maintained forever. Self is always useless, is always judged by God, and should therefore continually be delivered to death. How very sad that the righteousness which we forsook at the time of first believing in the Lord is once more welcomed not too long a while afterwards. What we acknowledged as useless self is gradually becoming active once again.

God's original intention for us after we are saved is that step by step we should come into deeper knowledge of our corruption as well as into greater rejection of our own righteousness. The attitude we took towards our selves at the time of salvation is only the first step in the perfect work of God. He wants to see such work go deeper and deeper until we believers are completely delivered from the dominion of self. What a pity that Christians should ruin the work of God.

The first work of the Holy Spirit in a believer after he is saved is to lead him to know himself so as to induce him to obey the will of God and to deny what comes from himself. He is to learn to trust in God completely. But how difficult this lesson is! To know one's self is to be deprived of glory; to deny one's self is to make oneself suffer. So that in reality a believer is not too eager to know himself and therefore he does not know himself that well; indeed, he will ignorantly deem himself as trustworthy. Now because of the believer's unwillingness to have such self-knowledge, the Holy Spirit is not able to reveal to him his true character in the sight of God. As a result, the Lord is forced to use some painful means to make a believer know himself. And the means most frequently used is to let the believer fail.

As the failures in the wilderness enabled the children of Israel to know their heart, so similar failures will cause believers today to know how wretched they are in themselves. Because of their self-reliance and the viewing of themselves as talented, able and powerful, they lack the heart for complete dependence on God. Hence God lets them fail in their attempts. They will realize how undependable they are when their works do not produce true and lasting fruit.

How believers regard themselves as naturally very patient, kind, gentle and pure. To counteract this self-delusion God permits many things to happen in their lives to take away their patience, kindness, gentleness and purity so that they shall know that nothing is dependable which comes out of the natural self. How Christians view themselves as loving God, boasting of their perfect consecration towards the Lord and their diligent labor on His behalf! God allows the world and the people of the world to woo them in such a way that they are either secretly tempted or openly backslidden. And thus will they know how vulnerable is their love for God. Or believers may think of themselves as totally for the Lord and holding nothing for themselves. In response, God causes them to experience praises and accolades of men in order to show them how they subtly steal His glory and seek for men's exaltation. Then, too, sometimes when believers make a little progress in the spiritual life, they are prone to think of themselves as now being victorious and sanctified. But just as these Christians are indulging in some such self-satisfaction, God permits them to fail and to sin exactly as do other people—or even worse than others. With the result that they know they are no better than anybody else.

At the risk of being misunderstood, I would like to say this to you: God would rather have His children sin than do good. Again, please do not misunderstand my word here. I am not, by these words, advising you to sin, because the Lord takes no pleasure in sin. But since believers are so self-reliant, self-boasting and self-satisfied—being full of their own thoughts, feelings and actions—God would rather see them sin than do good. Otherwise, they shall never know themselves nor shall they ever be delivered from that pitiable, sometimes laughable, yet abhorrent self life.

We should know to what extent God wants us to reach forward. Where does He save us *from* and *to where* will He save us? It is quite true we shall not go to hell but go to heaven. But is this all which God has purposed for us? No, He wishes to save us to the extent of our being wholly delivered from ourselves and of our entering fully into His life so that we will no longer live by the life of the soul. In His eyes there is nothing more unclean than "self"—it being the mother of all sins. Self is God's greatest enemy, because self always declares independence from Him. He therefore looks upon all self as extremely unclean, totally unacceptable and absolutely useless. What basically is self? Whatever man possesses and is able to do without seeking, waiting and depending on God is self.

Although the Lord hates "self" so much, the attitude of believers towards it is quite different. They delight in depending on self, cherishing self, and glorying in self. They are ignorant of their true self; and neither do they know how unclean and corrupt and weak the self is in God's eyes. They lack the divine insight into the matter. In short, they do not know themselves. If in such a situation they should make much progress, experiencing an increasing number of successes and victories, their self life will be nourished and grow bigger and it will thus become harder to deny. Each time they do a good deed, they drift a step further from the life of God. A little more power of their own means a little more distance away from the Holy Spirit. More success results in more glory to self, hence prolonging the evil life of self.

It is for this reason that I said earlier that God would rather have the believers sin than do good: because the more they sin, the more they shall realize their undependability; the weaker they are, the more they shall see the vanity of self; and the more they fall, the clearer they shall perceive their helplessness and hopelessness. God would rather see believers sin at such a time in their walk because sinning will enable them to know themselves more thoroughly and to depend on the Lord.

God has no other aim than to lead you to the end of yourself that you may know yourself. This is thus the explanation for why, when sometimes you have struggled to overcome, you nevertheless have failed. Oh how you cried, you strove, you fought, you pursued, you prayed, you worked and labored, you employed all kinds of means to overcome sin and reach holiness; yet you ended up in defeat. Although at times you did experience a little victory, such victory was only temporary. You tried your best to sustain it, but it flew away like a bird. You concluded that you were worse than all, and therefore you could not gain the victory. Such experiences find their meaning in the fact that God was leading you to know your own self. It is not because you were too corrupt to gain a victory; rather, it was because you were not corrupt enough in your own eyes to win the victory. You ought to recognize that it is you yourself who cried, it was you who struggled and fought, it was you yourself who prayed and pursued, that it was you who worked and labored. You were the one active, and it was all for your own self.

How much do you really depend on God? Do you truly know yourself as irredeemable and are thus ready to rely on God? What is the motive for your struggling and pursuing anyway? Is it not for your own self? Yes, you seek to overcome sin and to strive at holiness; but for what? Is it not for the sake of giving *you* more joy, more glory, and more ground for boasting? Unless you come to acknowledge your own weakness and deceitfulness, you will continue to fail and fall until you recognize that you are powerless and deserve no honor.

God wants you to be united with Him and to depend on Him in all things so that you may do His will and glorify Him. But since you do not know your real character as evidenced by the fact that you continue to consider yourself good and able, you will naturally not rely on God and thus fail to render glory to Him. You will be self-reliant and self-glorifying. Even now you still do not know how weak you actually are. Hence God allows you to be repeatedly defeated. And with each defeat it tells you you are weak.

Yet you insist on not believing; you still refuse to despair of yourself; you instead continue to be full of hope. You conclude that that defeat of yours was due to the lack of exerting yourself. If you exert yourself more the next time, you say to yourself, then you will no doubt overcome. Many have been your defeats, and many have been the times that you encountered ups and downs. Yet you remain ignorant of how weak you truly are. Up to the very present hour, you are not ready to learn the lesson which God has designed for you. You are still planning your last effort for gaining the final victory. Having suffered so many defeats, why are you not yet totally despairing of yourself and wholly casting yourself upon God? When will you expect nothing from yourself, committing yourself completely into God's hand? Oh! When that finally *does* happen, you will depend on Him without planning or doing anything out from yourself. But because you have not yet learned your lesson, you will have to incur greater and more defeats to give you the self-knowledge which will impel you to cease from your own work so that God may deliver you.

We all know that no rescuer dares to rescue a person who has just fallen into the water with the likelihood of drowning. For at that moment the strength of the fallen person is very strong—perhaps even stronger than usual. When the rescuer approaches the drowning person, the latter may try to wrap himself around the rescuer and keep him from swimming. With the result that both may sink and be drowned. Consequently, a wise rescuer will wait until the drowning person has struggled enough in the water on his own and begun to give up struggling. Only then will the rescuer approach the fallen one and bring him to safety.

In like manner God today allows His children to struggle and struggle till they realize how futile is their effort since they are merely getting themselves into a more perilous position. The Lord will wait until their strength is exhausted and they themselves judge that they are dying. At that moment, their thought runs something like this: If God does not deliver me, I cannot maintain my lot even for a minute; if God does not save, I will certainly die! Not until that very moment will God stretch out His saving hand. Whenever a believer ceases to trust in himself, God will wholly save him at that moment. For the Lord has no other aim than to show the believer that he is absolutely useless in divine life and work. Apart from depending on God, the believer has no life nor work.

Oh how deceitful we can be! How tenaciously interested we are in ourselves! Who can tell how many believers are living today by their deceitful self! Many are those who take "self" as the guiding principle of living. Almost everything is *for* self and almost everything proceeds *from* self. Such believers are much more dangerous than other people. It appears that in all things they cannot escape from self. If they learn to know one more thing, it is for the sake of glorifying self. This is not only true in spiritual things, it is also true in worldly things. Everything becomes a ground for elevating the self. Oh, who can fully understand the deceitfulness of the flesh? God must break and wreck such believers. He will give them no easy environment lest their ego be nourished. He will deal with them in severe circumstances lest they be boastful. He will let them know what their inner motive really is by allowing them to be defeated so that in defeat they may examine themselves and realize how much in their ordinary days they are for *themselves* and *not* for the glory of God.

For forty long years God led the children of Israel through the wilderness. He let them fall and sin *many* times, with this one purpose in view: that they might know themselves. In the same way today what God has been doing in your life is for the purpose of causing you to know your real image. Your past defeats ought to have already convinced you of the absolute vanity of yourself; yet to this present moment you insist on clinging to your precious self! Because of this, God is compelled to keep you in the wilderness longer that you may have more experience of wilderness defeats so as to realize at last how utterly corrupt, vain and weak you are before God. And if you still do not learn your lesson today, you will have to continue in defeat.

What is God's purpose in having given the law to men through these thousands of years? It has been given not for men to keep but for men to violate, for the law was established for transgressions. Do not be shocked by this statement, for concerning the law this is the purpose of God, as is amply demonstrated in the Scriptures. God has known long before that men are corrupt beyond remedy, and He willed long ago that we should be saved freely by His grace. He knows we are so corrupt that we cannot bring anything to Him for acceptance. But He additionally knows that we do not realize this ourselves. He therefore employs ways and means to teach us in order that we too may know about ourselves what He has always known. Only after we recognize our corruption will we ever accept His grace.

Now one means He employs is the law, which He requires us to keep. If we are good, we will certainly keep it; but if we are corrupt, we will with equal certainty break it. It may therefore be said that the very breaking of the law reveals that we are corrupt, that our inability to do what the law demands proves that our flesh is weak (see Rom. 8.3). When people see that they are so weak as to be unable to satisfy the demands of divine law, they will finally despair of themselves, give up any thought of being saved by works, and entirely trust in the grace of God. Hence the Bible declares: "What then is the law? It was added because of transgressions"—that is to say, it was added to reveal the corruption of men—"till the seed should come to whom the promise hath been made" (Gal. 3.19)—this latter clause referring to the Lord Jesus and His salvation.

We believers know that we cannot be saved by works but only by grace. But do we know why? It is because we are so corrupt, weak and unclean that we cannot accomplish the righteousness of God nor keep His law, and consequently we do not have any good works to show but must depend on grace. God in saving us by grace tells us that we are so utterly corrupt that He has no other recourse but to give His grace. And when we at last entered through the gate of salvation we very well knew how helpless we were.

Why then is it that today you begin to think of yourself as so good? Why is it that you have not learned the lesson God has been teaching through the law to His followers throughout these thousands of years? Alas, you still do not know yourself!

In our public preaching and testimony, we have paid special attention to the principle of the cross. But keep in mind that the cross is not a kind of magic power which will deliver you from all your sins by the mere calling on it. Except you willingly accept the principle of the cross, you will not see it work in your life. The cross is a principle, and the principle of the cross is to deny self and depend on God. If you are ignorant of the utter corruption of your real self, you will not receive the help of the cross in delivering you from sin when you expect its power in an emergency.

A person may say: "I am surprised that I could commit such a sin." This reveals that that individual does not know himself. He has no knowledge as to how corrupt he is, as to how he is capable of committing any sin. Let it be understood that apart from the new life which God has given us at the time of new birth, we ourselves are no better than anybody else. Let us acknowledge that every man has the possibility of being a robber, and every woman, a prostitute The reason why some are not is due to a different environment. I do not hesitate to confess that the seed of every sin is within me and that I could commit any sin if the life of God does not rule in me.

How many tears are shed today not for the sake of sin, but for the sake of "self" that is incapable of reaching the expected goodness of a believer. Much seeking, prayers and faith appear to be directed towards God, yet within all these endeavors is most likely the anticipation of self-good. And hence God permits you to be defeated again and again so that you may see finally the utter corruption of the flesh. And once your weakness is proven by such defeats, it is hoped by God that you may know your true self, forsake it and turn to trust in Him.

Each defeat ought to give you a little more knowledge of yourself. Each failure should show you a little more of your weakness. Each sin should make you expect less of yourself and make you more willing to forsake your self. Yet often every fall only brings in more struggle and fight. Self is increased in strength instead of it being decreased. How vain it is for anyone to confess with the lips and even cry out for help if he fails to accept the principle of the cross in judging self.

Have not the Scriptures already warned us of such error? Romans 6 speaks of our co-death with Christ; Romans 7 speaks of the battle between the new and the old lives; and Romans 8 speaks of the victory in the Holy Spirit. With co-death, we ought to be victorious. Yet why is it that after we have known and accepted the truth of Romans 6, we still cannot be victorious? It is because we lack the defeat of Romans 7. Both verse 6 and verse 11 of Romans 6 tell us that the death of our "self" is a fact. Why, then, do many — believing in this truth — fail to experience the victory of Romans 8? It is because they have not failed enough. God will lead us through the defeat of Romans 7 many times over till finally we are forced to confess: "I am carnal, sold under sin. . . . I know that in me, that is, in my flesh, dwelleth no good thing" (Rom. 7.14b,18a). And such an experience is true self knowledge.

God will let a believer fall until he willingly acknowledges, "I am sold under sin! There is no good in me!" Not till then will he know that except a power comes from outside, he is hopeless and helpless. But then he will cry out: "Wretched man that I am! Who shall deliver me?" (7.24) When he really perceives how corrupt he is, he will then know and acknowledge that unless Christ rescues him he cannot overcome sin.

At the beginning of Romans 8 the co-death of Romans 6 is again mentioned as the means for total victory. Oh, we are familiar with the salvation through co-death, and we earnestly expect the glory of victory. Yet the problem today is knowing self.

Our past defeats are not a few, yet we are unwilling to
know self in such defeats; instead, we try our best to
improve and cover our self. If only we were willing to
examine those past defeats in the light of God's holiness, we would surely know what kind of people we
are. If we are ready to go a step further by denying
self, God will lead us into the restfulness of Canaan.

Naturally we do have a little knowledge of ourselves, and in our past experiences we have been led
by God to know something of our corruption. But I
am honestly afraid that the knowledge of many concerning self is not deep enough. Let us not be fearful
of knowing ourselves too clearly! Although self is
quite ugly and very fearful, so abominable and so
hateful, we still must know. We must never stop short
and conclude that we already know the self thoroughly: we are far, far away yet in knowing our self!

Knowing the self is a lifelong lesson for a believer.
In order to arrive at this purpose of God a stubborn
believer may have to go through defeats which others
do not have or need. He may even conclude that the
Lord is especially hard on him, not realizing that this
is due to his stronger tie to his "self." For not long after he gains a victory, he has begun to become self-
important once again. He ceases to trust in the Lord
with fear and trembling as before and instead com-
mences to glorify himself afresh. So back to failure
God sends him once more. How many believers do indeed have victories up to the present. But they somehow never seem to be able to learn the lesson God is
teaching them of true self-knowledge.

Oh, do let us see that outside of self-knowledge,

self-examination and self-denial, there is really no way to spiritual life. If we would constantly judge ourselves because of knowing ourselves, we would avoid many defeats and achieve God's purpose.

Today all who (1) follow their own will, (2) rely on their own strength and (3) glorify their own self are people who do not know themselves. But once anyone is thoroughly broken by God, that person shall see himself as abominable and hateful. He will not dare initiate anything or dare to do anything in his own strength. He will instead wait for God's will in all things and depend on God's power. In the event there is any achievement he will dare not be self-conceited because he knows he is unworthy of any glory. May the Lord lead us all into such an experience and thus bring glory to Him.

7 | How Is Your Heart?

Let the words of my mouth and the meditation of my heart be acceptable in thy sight, O Jehovah, my rock, and my redeemer. (Ps. 19.14)

When he had removed him, he raised up David to be their king; to whom also he bare witness and said, I have found David the son of Jesse, a man after my heart, who shall do all my will. Of this man's seed hath God according to promise brought unto Israel a Saviour, Jesus. (Acts 13.22,23)

One

Quoted here are two Scripture passages related to David. Psalm 19.14 is his prayer and Acts 13.22,23 speaks of him as a man. In his prayer David mentions the words of his mouth and then the meditation of his heart. He seeks to have his inward thought as well as his outward words acceptable to God. For the words of the mouth are the expression of the inward thought. Hence the heart is the principal problem. Whether or not the outward words are correct is not the central issue, nor is it the correctness of outward attitude. The real problem lies in the intent of the heart. The thought and intent of the heart is the issue that must not be neglected. For this reason David prays to have the meditation of his heart acceptable to God as much as to have the words of his mouth acceptable. His prayer is for God's acceptance of his inward desire. Hence Paul testifies that David is a man after God's heart (Acts 13).

What kind of man is a man after God's own heart? It is the one who allows God to touch his heart. If a person will not allow Him to touch his heart, he can hardly be a man of God's own heart.

Many Christians tend to ask: Am I not right in doing so and so? Am I not right in speaking thus? Am I not correct in such expression? Yet the essential question does not lie in whether their doing or speaking or expressing is right or not; it rests instead upon what is the root of their so doing, speaking or expressing. Even though a person is alright outwardly, he may still have a problem with his heart. What God will ask about and touch will concern itself with that one's heart. It is for this reason that He permits many things to happen—wave upon wave—in the lives of His children. He uses these things to touch their hearts by exposing what is there.

Two

In the Bible we observe that the way David sojourns through life is by way of the cross, and the life he lives is the life of the cross. The New Testament begins with two persons in particular: one is Abraham and the other is David (see Matt. 1.1, 2, 6). This is because these two men have brought in the Lord Jesus. They have brought God from heaven to earth. God must find persons such as these two before He has a way to come from heaven to earth.

We know that Abraham is the father of faith. Throughout his life he walks the way of faith. Only this way can bring God to earth. On the other hand, the way David travels through life is by way of the cross. His life is a life of the cross. He not only brings God into the midst of men, he also causes God to rule over men.

If you live in faith, you have the way of bringing God into the midst of men; if you live in the cross, you will enable God to reign over men. Were God's children more willing to go the way of the cross and to bear the cross, God would no doubt have more dominion over men. Unless you live the life of the cross, God cannot reign in you. The special feature of David's life is displayed in his walking the pathway of the cross.

Three

What David encountered in his life was rather strange, but all those events revealed the condition of his heart. First of all, David was despised in his own family. When God sent Samuel to anoint a son of Jesse to be king over Israel, Jesse called in his many sons but neglected to summon David. Nevertheless, the heart of this youth was right, for he did not lose his proper relationship because of such negligence. God told Samuel: "Man looketh on the outward appearance, but Jehovah looketh on the heart" (1 Sam. 16.7b). The inward heart of David was acceptable to God, so he was chosen and used by Him.

After David killed Goliath he was put into a peculiar situation by God — for the women of Israel subsequently sang: "Saul hath slain his thousands, and David his ten thousands" (18.7b). Concerning these two clauses, it will be seen that the one was to test David and the other was to test Saul. It is said in Proverbs 27 that "a man is tried by his praise" (v.21). When people overly-praise you, closely notice whether you become proud; or if people under-praise you, watch whether you become jealous. How did these two declarations of the Israelitish women affect the hearts of David and Saul? We learn that David was not at all swayed by the shout, "He hath slain his ten thousands"; Saul, however, was touched deeply by the words that he had only slain his thousands. Obviously, Saul's jealous heart was being searched out greatly (1 Sam 18.6–9).

Suppose you and another brother do a certain thing together. What if someone tells you to your face what an excellent work that brother has done without mentioning you at all? At the least you will perhaps feel uncomfortable inside and a little unhappy. That little uncomfortableness and unhappy feeling proves that you are not wholly clean. Do you not repeatedly confess to yourself you did this for God and not for man? Yet the praising of somebody else involved shakes your heart and discloses the uncleanness within. Let us come to understand that many of the circumstances we are in—especially the attitudes of those who are near to us—test our heart. After David killed Goliath he became the hero of Israel, but then he was afflicted by Saul. During this long period of testing, he submitted himself under the hand of God and dared not do anything to bypass His hand. And thus was shown how clear and right was David's heart.

After David became king he was confronted with serious trials because of his great failure. His own son sought his life, and Shimei cursed him and cast stones at him. Concerning Shimei, how did David react? His heart was again as transparent as crystal. Said David: Shimei has done this "because Jehovah hath said unto him, Curse David" (see 2 Sam. 16.5-12). He was looking for the mercy of God. Oh, let us not think that all the happenings in our lives are for our loss. On the one hand, it is quite true that if our heart is not right we shall suffer loss; but if on the other hand our heart is right we shall be benefited greatly, for all such circumstances are arranged to prove what is in our heart. David's true heart condition is revealed through the testings of a life lived in the cross.

Four

Hence God's children must not only be careful about their speech and attitude; even more so, they should be careful about the thought and intent of their hearts. Frequently our outward expression does not necessarily reveal the inward condition. More often than not it is our inner feeling which betrays the real condition of our heart. How futile it is merely to keep a guard over our lips. If our heart is not right, sooner or later, it *will* be openly expressed—and often when we least expect it. An example of this would be our idle words spoken about other people. The more our heart is out towards God and the purer it is to Him, the less will be the idle words we shall utter. Every time we gossip and murmur against people we betray some irregularity in our heart. For if a person's heart were wholly towards God he would not say such idle words against other people.

A brother once said: "If a little brother sins against me, I can forgive him; but if a big brother sins against me, I cannot forgive him." Another brother who heard him say this looked at the chest of this brother and nodded his head continuously. What he meant by this gesture was: "Your heart! Your heart! In forgiving a little brother but in not forgiving a big brother, you expose what your heart is like. The fact that a little brother sins against you and is forgiven by you cannot at all expose your true heart condition; but when you refuse to forgive a big brother who sins against you, that really reveals what is in your heart." Through this incident, that brother's unforgiving heart was unveiled. Let us see that something small may not be burned by a single match but it will be completely consumed in a fiery furnace. This shows that this thing can be burned. Similarly speaking, a little brother was not able to test out this brother's heart, but a big brother was instrumental in bringing out what was truly his inward state.

If our heart is right, we will not be shaken by anybody, for we look only to God. David proved to be a man after God's own heart because in whatever environment God placed him his heart was kept in direct relationship with the Lord and not with men. David accepted everything from God's hand and tried to see things from His viewpoint. Let me repeat, that God uses circumstances to reveal our heart. May we therefore pray: "O Lord, let the words of my mouth and the meditations of my heart be acceptable in Your sight."

8 | Man's First Sin

Out of the ground made Jehovah God to grow every tree that is pleasant to the sight, and good for food; the tree of life also in the midst of the garden, and the tree of the knowledge of good and evil. (Gen. 2.9)

Jehovah God commanded the man, saying, Of every tree of the garden thou mayest freely eat: but of the tree of the knowledge of good and evil, thou shalt not eat of it: for in the day that thou eatest thereof thou shalt surely die. (Gen. 2.16,17)

The serpent said unto the woman, Ye shall not surely die: for God doth know that in the day ye eat thereof, then your eyes shall be opened, and ye shall be as God, knowing good and evil. And when the woman saw that the tree was good for food, and that it was a delight to the eyes, and that the tree was to be desired to make one wise, she took of the fruit thereof, and did eat; and she gave also unto her husband with her, and he did eat. And the eyes of them both were opened, and they knew that they were naked; and they sewed fig-leaves together, and made themselves aprons. And they heard the voice of Jehovah God walking in the garden in the cool of the day: and the man and his wife hid themselves from the presence of Jehovah God amongst the trees of the garden. (Gen. 3.4–8)

In this study we would like to see how man first sinned, and receive it as a warning for us today. For as the first sin was, so shall all the sins afterwards be. The sin which Adam committed is the same we all commit. So by knowing the first sin, we may understand all the sins in the world. For according to the view of the Bible, sin has but one principle behind it.

In every sin we can see "self" at work. Although people today classify sins into an untold number of categories, yet inductively speaking there is but one basic sin: all the thoughts and deeds which are sins are related to "self." In other words, though the number of sins in the world is indeed astronomical, the principle behind every sin is simply one—whatever is for self. All sins are committed for the sake of the self. If the element of self is missing, there will be no sin. Let us examine this point a little more closely.

What is pride? Is it not an exalting of self? What is jealousy? Is not jealousy a fear of being supplanted? What is emulation? Nothing less than a striving to excel others. What is anger? Anger is reacting against the loss the self suffers. What is adultery? It is following self's passions and lusts. What is cowardice? Is it not a caring for self's weakness? Now it is impossible to mention every sin, but if we were to examine all of them one by one, we would discover that the principle within each one is always the same: it is something that in some way is related to self. Wherever sin is, there is the activity of the self. And wherever self is active, there will be sin before God.

On the other hand, in examining the fruit of the Holy Spirit — which expresses Christian witness — we shall readily see the opposite: that they are none other than selfless acts. What is love? Love is loving others without thinking of self. What is joy? It is looking at God in spite of self. Patience is despising one's own hardship. Peace is disregarding one's loss. Gentleness is overlooking one's rights. Humility is forgetting one's merits. Temperance is the self under control. And faithfulness is self-restraint. As we examine every Christian virtue, we will discern that other than being delivered from self or being forgetful of self, a believer has no other virtue. The fruit of the Holy Spirit is determined by one principle alone: the losing of self totally.

Granted, I have only mentioned a few virtues and a few sins; but I trust they are sufficient to prove that sin is the following of self whereas virtue is the forgetting of self. If we understand these two principles, we can daily observe all the various sins and judge whether each one is related to self or not. But let me tell you plainly that apart from man being "selfless" there is no virtue and apart from his being "selfish" there is no sin. The self in man is the root of all evils.

In the passages we read at the beginning we are told there were two trees in the Garden of Eden and that Adam, through eating the fruit of the tree of the knowledge of good and evil, had brought sin into the world. Let us take a closer look at the two trees mentioned. I will use two words to represent the meaning of both trees. The meaning of the tree of the knowledge of good and evil is *independence,* and that of the tree of life is *trust.*

We will examine the tree of the knowledge of good and evil first. At the outset we should understand that eating the fruit of this tree is not by its action a very great sin. Adam did not commit adultery here, nor did he murder or do many other unclean sins. He merely ate the fruit of the tree of the knowledge of good and evil. Now although what Adam did was not some frightening sin, nonetheless, in eating the fruit of this tree he caused not only himself to fall but also his progeny, thus filling the world with sins. Even though the sin he committed was not hideous, nevertheless, most hideous sins have sprung from his not very hideous act. According to our logic, if man's first sin is in actual fact the "mother" of every sin in the world, that very first sin ought to be the most hideous of all. Yet what we see here is merely one man eating too much fruit. In one sense, then, it is innocuous in its appearance.

Why is this so? God regards Adam's sin as constituting the typical specimen of the countless sins to be committed by all men afterwards. He wants us to understand by this that no matter what the nature of Adam's sin is, that shall also be the nature of the multitudinous and varied sins the world will commit after Adam. Outwardly sin has the difference of being civil or rude, but its nature and principle always remain the same. Adam's sin is none other than following his own will. Since God had forbidden him to eat that particular fruit, he should have completely disregarded his own mind and obeyed. But he disobeyed God and ate the fruit after his own will. And thus did he sin. Hence Adam's sin was nothing less than acting outside of God and according to his own will. Though the sins committed by Adam's progeny greatly differed from his in outward forms (for there is not another person afterwards who can commit the same sin which Adam committed), yet in principle they have also acted according to self will, and therefore their sins are all the same in nature.

Is it a sin to know good and evil? Is it not virtuous to seek to know good and evil? For God knows good and evil (see Gen. 3.5, 22). Is it a sin to be like God? Is it not a commendable thing to seek to be like God? How is it, then, that this act of Adam's becomes the very root of all human sin and misery? For what reason? Although such action on the surface appears to be good, Adam acted without God's command or promise. And in trying to obtain this knowledge outside of God and according to his own self, Adam sinned. Do we now see the significance here of that word "independence"? All *independent* actions are sins. Adam had not trusted in God; he had not set himself aside in order to obey God; he had acted independently of God; and in order to obtain this knowledge he had proclaimed independence against God. And that is why the Lord declared that this was sin.

Therefore understand this fully, that it does not require the committing of many hideous and terrible sins to be reckoned as sinning. To God, all actions taken outside of Him are sins. "To be like God," for instance, is an excellent desire; but to attempt to do it without listening to God's command and waiting for God's time is sinful in His sight. How often we reckon evil things as sins but good things as righteousness. God, however, reckons things differently. Instead of differentiating good and evil by appearance, He looks into the way a thing is done. No matter how excellent it may appear to the world to be, whatever is done by the believer without seeking God's will, waiting for His time, or depending on His power (but done according to one's own mind, in hastiness, or by one's own ability) — such action is sinning in God's sight.

The Lord looks not at the good or evil of a thing. He looks instead to its source. He takes note by what power the thing is done. Apart from His own will, God is not satisfied with anything else. Apart from His own power, He is not interested in any other. Were it possible for a believer to do something better than the will of God, the latter would still condemn the action and consider the believer as having sinned.

Is it true that all your works and pursuits are according to God's will? Or are they simply your independent decision? Do your works originate with God? Or are they done according to your pleasure? All our independent actions, no matter how excellent or virtuous they may appear to be, are not acceptable to God. Everything done without clearly knowing the will of God is a sin in His eyes. Everything done without depending on Him is also sin.

Today's Christians are too capable in doing

things, they are too active and doing too many good things! Yet God does not look at how many good things you have done, He only concerns himself with how much is done because of His command. He does not inquire how much you labor for Him; He only asks how much you depend on Him. It is not in much activity that God is pleased; it is in how much you depend on Him. No matter how zealously you work for the Lord, your work will be futile if it is not done by Him in you. We ought to ask this of ourselves: Is the work I do done by the Lord in me, or is it merely myself doing the work? All works independent of Him are sinful works.

Please beware that we may even sin while saving souls. If we do not depend on God but trust in our own understanding and experience of the gospel, we will be sinning and not saving souls in the sight of God even if we have spent time and energy in persuading people to believe in the Lord! If instead of sensing our utter weakness and leaning entirely on the power of the Lord we try to edify saints on the strength of our knowledge of the Bible and our excellent speech, in God's eyes we will be sinning while preaching! However good they may seem to be to the public, all acts of love and compassion—if they are undertaken by our impulse or strength—are deemed to be sinful in God's sight. The Lord does not ask if we have done well; He only examines if we have trusted in Him. Whatever is done out of one's self will be burned up on that day at the judgment seat of Christ, and what is done out of God shall remain.

The meaning of the fruit of the tree of the knowledge of good and evil is none other than being active outside of God, seeking what is good according to one's thought, being in haste and unable to wait to obtain the knowledge which God has not yet given, and not trusting in the Lord but seeking advance in one's own way. These all can be summed up in one phrase: independence from God. And such was man's first sin. God is displeased with the man who departs from Him and moves independently. For He wants man to trust in Him.

The purpose of the Lord in saving man as well as in creating him is for man to trust in God. And such is the meaning of the tree of life: simply put, it is *trust*. "Of every tree of the garden thou mayest freely eat," said God to Adam; "but of the tree of the knowledge of good and evil, thou shalt not eat of it." Among all the trees whose fruit could be eaten, God especially mentioned the tree of life in stark contrast to the tree of the knowledge of good and evil. "The tree of life also in the midst of the garden, and the tree of the knowledge of good and evil." In taking note of God's mention particularly of the tree of life, we ought to realize that of all the edible trees, this one is the most important. This is what Adam should have eaten of first. Why is this so?

The tree of life signifies the life of God, the *un*created life of God. Adam is a *created* being, and therefore he does not possess such uncreated life. Though at this point he is still without sin, he nevertheless is only natural since he has not received the holy life of God. The purpose of God is for Adam to choose the fruit of the tree of life with his own volition so that he might be related to God in divine life. And thus Adam would move from simply being created by God to his being born of Him as well. What God requires of Adam is simply for him to deny his created, natural life and be joined to Him in divine life, thus living daily by the life of God. Such is the meaning of the tree of life. The Lord wanted Adam to live by that life which was not his originally.

Hence we have here the distinctive sense of dependence or trust. For when the created being lives by his created life, he does not need to be very dependent on God. This created life is autonomous and self-preserving. But for the created being to live by the life of the Creator, he has to be wholly dependent because the life he would then live by is not his but God's. He could not be independent of God but would have to maintain constant fellowship with Him and completely rely on Him. Such life is what Adam does not have in himself and so he must trust God to receive it. Moreover, such life—if received by Adam—is what he could not live out by his own effort; and therefore he would have to depend on God continuously in order to keep it. And thus the condition for keeping it would become the same condition for receiving it. Adam would have to depend on God day by day in order for him to live out this godly life in a practical way.

All this that has been said with regard to Adam is required of us by God as well. At the time of Adam the life of God and the life of man were both present in the garden. Today the divine life and the human life are both present within us. We who have believed in the Lord and are saved have been born again—that is to say, born of God; and thus we have a life relationship with God. The life of the created is in us, but so too is the life of the Creator. The current problem, then, is whether or not we live by the divine life —whether or not our lives are totally dependent on God. Just as our flesh cannot live if separated from its created life, so our spiritual life is not able to be lived if separated from the life of the Creator.

God wants us to have no activity outside of Him. He wishes us to die to ourselves and be dependent on Him as though we cannot move without Him. He does not like our initiating anything without His command. He is pleased if we really sense helplessness in ourselves and thus rely on Him wholeheartedly. We ought to resist all actions independent of God. Works which are done without prayer and waiting, without seeking and knowing clearly the divine will, without entirely trusting God, and without examining our conscience to determine if there is any self or impurity mixed in: all are from our own selves and are sinful in God's sight.

The Lord does not ask how good is your work; He only asks who does the work? He will not be moved by the little good you or I do. He is never satisfied with anything except *His* work. You may be actively engaged and labor hard, you may even be said to have suffered for the sake of Christ and His church; but if you are not sure it is God who wants you to do the work, or if you do not fully realize your own ignorance and incompetency so that in much fear and trembling you cast yourself upon the Lord, then like

Adam you will be sinning in the sight of God. Oh, do cease from your own work! Do not imagine that whatever thing is good is something you can do. You may labor and endeavor according to your own pleasure, but you will have little if any spiritual usefulness.

We all know that an unbeliever, no matter how good his conduct is, cannot be saved. Do we not know many unbelievers whose conduct is commendably good? They are kind, loving, humble, patient; they often surpass ordinary Christians in virtue. Why is it that notwithstanding such enviable conduct they still are not saved? Because all this good comes from their natural self life, and it therefore cannot obtain God's approval. God is pleased only with what belongs to Him, what comes from himself. Consequently, no unbeliever can please God with the good deeds of his own.

Yet the same is true for the believer. Do we think we can please the Lord with the good and zealous works of our own? We ought to realize that except for the life which God has given us, there is not the slightest difference between *our* self and the self of the unbelievers. These selves are absolutely the same. The created life of a sinner and the created life of a saint have no difference one from another. If the good deeds done through this created life by the *un*believers are rejected by God, so will the good done through this created life by the believers be rejected by God too.

How sad that we so easily forget the lesson we had learned before! When we first believed in the Lord

Jesus, God convicted us by His Holy Spirit that our righteousness was of no use before Him. After we are saved, though, we somehow turn into imagining that now our own righteousness is useful and pleasing to God. We ought to know better, that our being saved and born again has not improved or changed our old life one whit. Except for the newly obtained life of God, our old self remains just the same.

The principle which we learn at the time of regeneration should be maintained continually. Since we as unbelievers were not saved by our independent works, so we as believers will not gain the approval of God by our independent actions either. Whatever is done without depending upon God is displeasing to Him. Whether it comes from sinner or saint, independent action is rejected by God.

You may boast of how much you as a believer have done, how much you have labored, even how much blessing and fruit you have experienced; still, in the eyes of God these are but dead works having no usefulness at all. For all of them are done by yourself and not by His working in you.

How very hard it is to depend on God! How difficult it is for the wise to trust! How arduous for the talented to rely on the Divine. Oftentimes we become active without waiting on God for special strength. For us to deny our talent, to become utterly helpless before God and to not depend on talent but completely on the Lord, is most difficult. The Lord wants us to deny ourselves and our power and to acknowledge our weakness and helplessness in every word and deed. Except the supply of God comes forth, we cannot say a word or do a work. Only in such manner as this does He want us to depend on Him. For what we have in ourselves will invariably lead us away from God. Our talent, wisdom, power and knowledge all tend to strengthen our self-confidence to the loss of our trust in Him. Unless we purposely and persistently deny them, we will never rely on God.

When a child is small, he leans on his parents for everything; but once he grows up he possesses such power and wisdom in himself that he seeks independence instead of dependence. Our God desires us to have a permanent relationship with Him as children so that we may continuously trust in Him.

Do you think that you now have power? That you have already been sanctified? That you have already been filled permanently with the Holy Spirit? That your works have already produced fruits? If so, such ways of thinking will deprive you of a heart of dependence. You need to maintain the attitude and posture of being helpless before men in order to really advance in the way of God. If you allow your self to creep in subtly so that you consider yourself as having all things, you should realize that you will not rely on God anymore.

I who am now speaking to you have absolutely no assurance as to my future. I do not know if I shall still be preaching the gospel next year at this time. Unless God keeps me to this time next year I may not be able to serve; nay, I may not even follow Christ. I speak this out of an anguished heart, for I know I have no way to keep myself. Except I am kept by God, I confess I am not even capable of standing in today's humble place. I recall how I was on the verge of parting with Christ many times from the day of my becoming a believer to this present moment, but I praise God for keeping me.

Let me tell you that except by leaning on God and trusting Him moment by moment, I do not know of any way to live a sanctified life. If we do not rely on the Lord we cannot know how long we may continue with Him. Without depending on God we can do nothing, not even can we live as Christians for a single day.

Do we really feel this way now? Or do we still have a little power by which to sustain ourselves and to succeed in many things? Be it known to all that self-reliance is the enemy of dependence on God. God must bring us to our end so that we know there is no good in us. Were it not for His grace we would be defeated on every side. We need to come to the place where we know ourselves as absolutely wretched and without strength. We dare not be self-reliant, nor do we dare to take any independent action outside of God. We are to continue to prostrate ourselves before Him in fear and trembling, and to seek for His grace. Otherwise, our nature will usually cause us to think of ourselves as competent, thus delighting ourselves in activities and refusing to depend on God.

As I look back through the years I can see that many of the brethren whom I knew in the early days have fallen away. I still remember once being told by one of them: "Sir, we now know the Scriptures you teach. We have greatly progressed and are not too far from your workers." What self-reliance! But where are these brothers today? I also recall another brother telling me recently: "Brother Nee, if I do not know anything else I know at least the teachings of the Bible . . ." When I heard this, I knew immediately that this brother was in serious danger. Today he too has departed from the straight path. How many similar tragedies we may recall in our lifetime. One chief reason for such tragedies is this: self-reliance. The fact of the matter is that self-reliance is the cause of all defeats.

What God wants us to know today about our self is its absolute undependability. He wants us to confess that we are weak and useless at all times. He wants us to be aware of what we were never aware of before—that is to say, He wants us to be conscious of our utter helplessness and to admit that if it were not because of His keeping power, we could not stand a single moment, that if it were not because of His strengthening, we could not do a thing. May we be broken by the Lord today so that we do not and dare not take any independent action or harbor any attitude outside of Him. Otherwise, vanity and defeat will be the determined end. May God have mercy upon us all.

9 | Take the Helmet of Salvation

Out of the ground made Jehovah God to grow every tree that is pleasant to the sight, and good for food; the tree of life also in the midst of the garden, and the tree of the knowledge of good and evil. . . . But of the tree of the knowledge of good and evil, thou shalt not eat of it: for in the day that thou eatest thereof thou shalt surely die. (Gen. 2.9,17)

When the woman saw that the tree was good for food, and that it was a delight to the eyes, and that the tree was to be desired to make one wise, she took of the fruit thereof, and did eat; and she gave also unto her husband with her, and he did eat. And the eyes of them both were opened, and they knew that they were naked; and they sewed fig-leaves together, and made themselves aprons. (Gen. 3.6,7)

Our glory is this, the testimony of our conscience, that in holiness and sincerity of God, not in fleshly wisdom but in the grace of God, we behaved ourselves in the world, and more abundantly to you-ward. (2 Cor. 1.12)

Take the helmet of salvation, and the sword of the Spirit, which is the word of God. (Eph. 6.17)

And that ye be renewed in the spirit of your mind. (Eph. 4.23)

Be not fashioned according to this world: but be ye transformed by the renewing of your mind, that ye may prove what is the good and acceptable and perfect will of God. (Rom. 12.2)

They that are after the flesh mind the things of the flesh; but they that are after the Spirit the things of the Spirit. For the mind of the flesh is death; but the mind of the Spirit is life and peace. (Rom. 8.5,6)

One

In the midst of all the trees in the Garden of Eden there were both the tree of life and the tree of the knowledge of good and evil. God had commanded Adam: "Of every tree of the garden thou mayest freely eat: but of the tree of the knowledge of good and evil, thou shalt not eat of it: for in the day that thou eatest thereof thou shalt surely die" (Gen. 2.16b, 17). This indicates to us how contrary these two trees are. On the one hand is the tree of life, on the other is the tree of the knowledge of good and evil. We may therefore say that one is the tree of life and the other is the tree of death, for in eating of the tree of the knowledge of good and evil man would die.

We can notice a tremendous effect upon the lives

of Adam and Eve after they sinned: they gained in knowledge; for having eaten of that fruit, they then knew good and evil. In other words, the first subjective effect upon man in his fall was that his mind was enlarged in its capacity to function. Before the fall, man had a certain kind of mind; but after the fall, his mind began to contain a large portion of things which were originally purposed by God for him eventually to have — but not in the way men at that time obtained those things. For this reason Paul mentions in Ephesians 6.17 that the believer is to "take the helmet of salvation." This word attests to the need for the deliverance of the human mind. Many after they believe in the Lord Jesus have their lives changed, but their heads still need to be delivered. If their heads are undelivered, they will be without covering in time of spiritual conflict. Hence it is of the utmost importance for us to take the helmet of salvation.

There is a rather awesome problem among God's children: we may encounter many good-hearted and well-behaved people, but they carry with them heads which still belong to the old creation. To put it another way, their life is the life of Christ but their head is the head of Adam. This curtails their ability to know the will of God. Therefore, in measuring the spiritual life of a person, we need only measure his head. To the degree that his head is delivered, to that degree is he delivered from Adam and hence delivered from the old creation. The basic difference between living in the old and living in the new creation is seen in the relationship between one's head and God.

Two

"Not in fleshly wisdom but in the grace of God, we behaved ourselves" (2 Cor. 1.12b). How we need to ask God to deliver us from being clever in ourselves. The principle of Christian living is to rely on the will of God and not on one's cleverness, to depend on the grace of God and not on our own wisdom. This is a lesson we need to learn.

Suppose some action is put before you, but you do not know whether to do it this way or that, or not at all. You have no idea which is right. So you begin to deliberate on the effect of whichever action you may take. If you do it this way or that, what will people say? You therefore try to be clever. How? To say or to do that which will meet the least problem and avoid the most opposition. By following this policy it means you have forgotten that God's children do not live on earth by human cleverness. To be a Christian is really quite simple. You merely ask one thing: "God, what do You want me to do?"

It is clear that the tree of the knowledge of good and evil is still among the children of God today. Many are still feeding on its fruit daily. They do not eat of the tree of life. On the contrary, they do not cease asking, Which is better? — a question which arises from the tree of the knowledge of good and evil. Yet Paul tells us that today our life before God is most simple, for we do not lean on fleshly wisdom but on the grace of God. We are responsible for this one thing only: to do God's will.

Three

"Be ye transformed by the renewing of your mind, that ye may prove what is the good and acceptable and perfect will of God" (Rom. 12.2b).

Let every one of us remember that what we are responsible for is doing the will of God, and what God is responsible for is seeing to it that we experience the right consequence after we have done His will. We are prone to seek the pleasant way. Yet in this very connection, we find that the Son of God traveled on a most rugged road while on earth, He made himself responsible for doing God's will, and God in turn was responsible for giving Him the rugged road. When we testify that a Christian's fleshly wisdom is totally useless, we do not suggest that he should go ahead to do foolish things. For neither his fleshly wisdom nor his own foolishness is of any use to God. God does not need our folly, just as He does not need our wisdom. Not all foolish things are right; only things which issue from the divine will are right. We must perceive such a distinction. We are not in any way right when we deliberately say some foolish words or do some foolish things. What we are held accountable for is doing the will of God. Whatever the Lord wants me to do, that I do. But as to its result, that is His responsibility, not yours and mine.

Hence we must ask God to deliver us from our head: that our head may be saved by our taking the helmet of salvation. Whenever we encounter anything, we must first confess to God: "God, my head or my cleverness is not the principle of my Christian living. All that matters to me is to seek Your will." This does not mean that you need to pretend to be a fool. Let us say again that God has no more use for the fool than He does for the wise. We only insist that as Christians live in this world they are not to live by the deliberation of their heads but by proving what is the good and acceptable and perfect will of God.

The thinking of some people's heads is like a merchant's way of thinking. Whatever thing comes his way, his first reaction is to compute his personal gain or loss. This trait is true in spiritual things as well as in secular things. Such a head needs to be warned. For in spiritual things, the deciding factor is not personal gain or loss but the will of God. Oh do let us see that we have only one principle by which we can live, and that principle is "in the grace of God" — in doing the will of God.

Four

"Ye be renewed in the spirit of your mind" (Eph. 4.23). This means that the human mind needs renewal. Romans 12 gives the same injunction: "Be ye transformed by the renewing of your mind." The result is that "ye may prove what is the good and acceptable and perfect will of God." After your mind is renewed you may prove what the will of God is. So that knowing or not knowing the will of God is not a matter of method but a matter of person. Many are acquainted with the method of knowing God's will but their person is not right; consequently, they cannot know His will.

What kind of person may know God's will? The one whom God has delivered from brain power. Your mind must be renewed before you may prove what God's will is. Keep this ever before you: that the most vigorous part of man's natural life is his thinking apparatus. Some people may have their natural strength in their will while others may have theirs in their emotion. But more people have their natural strength in their head. When you meet a person with a vigorous mind, you meet his head. As you approach him, his thought begins to flow. His thought is bigger than his spirit. He seems to be extremely clever, for his character is reflected in his thought. If this that is his strength is not broken by the Lord, he will have no way of knowing the will of God. Accordingly we must ask the Lord to cause us not to trust in the power of our thinking.

A person may continuously confess how wrong his flesh or natural life is, yet all the while he cherishes his thought and opinions. Though he admits his weakness with his mouth, in his heart he is still full of his own thoughts and cleverness. He considers his view to be superior to that of others and his way to be better than that of others. His cleverness has not been broken by the Lord and his thought has not been dealt with. Because of this, he has no way of knowing the will of God. There are people whose lips are full of God's will, but in actuality they know nothing of it. Let us be reminded that if a person is not right, he cannot possibly know the divine will. The Lord must do a basic work of the cross in believers' lives, especially in renewing their thoughts. He will so break them that they can no longer reckon themselves as more clever or better than the rest. After their head has been dealt with, they may then prove and know what the will of God is.

The problem often lies in substituting God's will with man's thought. Our head therefore needs deliverance. A person who does not know the cross does not know the will of God. Hence the whole matter comes down once again to the necessity of the cross. Do you really know how the cross deals with your natural life? Do you have any idea as to how God deals with you as a person? One day when through the grace of the Lord you are brought to the place where you see your untrustworthiness and admit how undependable is your thought so that you dare not believe in yourself nor treasure your natural strength, then many things will become clear. As your natural life is dealt with by God, you will begin to be clear on His will.

Five

"They that are after the flesh mind the things of the flesh; but they that are after the Spirit the things of the Spirit. For the mind of the flesh is death; but the mind of the Spirit is life and peace" (Rom. 8.5, 6). What is the mind of the flesh? It has one chief characteristic: believing in oneself as all-knowing and all-capable. The mind of the Spirit in a believer has its chief characteristic too: not believing in himself nor daring to say or do anything but always being in fear and trembling. The mind of the flesh is constantly busy and swift, self-wise, and restless. And the result is death. The mind of the Spirit is not controlled by fleshly wisdom but is governed by the command of God, it having no confidence in the flesh nor daring to follow its own idea, with the result being life and peace. Our head needs to be delivered so that we will no longer be directed by fleshly thought but be guided by spiritual will instead.

Six

"Not in fleshly wisdom but in the grace of God, we behaved ourselves in the world, and more abundantly to you-ward" (2 Cor. 1.12b). Notice this last phrase, "more abundantly to you-ward." The Corinthians were clever people, but Paul declared that we should not live in fleshly wisdom but in the grace of God, and this more abundantly towards others like the clever Corinthians. Praise the Lord, we will not match our cleverness with clever people. The more calculating others are, the less cleverness we use; for we live by the grace of God. Especially in the things of God and of the church, we are determined not to use human wisdom nor human cleverness.

We therefore must learn the lesson of never putting our worldly brain into spiritual matters. We are not sure if such a worldly brain is effective in other matters, but we *are* sure of this one thing: that a worldly brain is absolutely useless in spiritual matters.

Worldly methods and tactics, worldly maneuvering and cleverness may produce results in other areas, but in the spiritual realm they are totally ineffective. In the house of God it is not man's hand or wisdom that counts but rather the will of God. Here it is not what man says or thinks but what the Lord says. We will ask God: "God, what pattern do You want to show us? For apart from Your revealed pattern we cannot entertain any other."

Let us learn to do God's will and not depend on our own cleverness. When we do the will of God, we look to Him to carry us through whatever problem we may encounter in the process. And thereafter we ask God to cause us to live not in fleshly wisdom but in His grace in doing His will.

TITLES YOU
WILL WANT TO HAVE

by Watchman Nee

Basic Lesson Series
Volume 1—A Living Sacrifice
Volume 2—The Good Confession
Volume 3—Assembling Together
Volume 4—Not I, But Christ
Volume 5—Do All to the Glory of God
Volume 6—Love One Another

The Church and the Work
Volume 1—Assembly Life
Volume 2—Rethinking the Work
Volume 3—Church Affairs

The Spirit of the Gospel
The Life That Wins
From Glory to Glory
The Spirit of Judgment
From Faith to Faith
The Lord My Portion
Aids to "Revelation"
Grace for Grace
The Better Covenant
A Balanced Christian Life
The Mystery of Creation
The Messenger of the Cross
Full of Grace and Truth—Volume 1
Full of Grace and Truth—Volume 2
The Spirit of Wisdom and Revelation
Whom Shall I Send?
The Testimony of God
The Salvation of the Soul
The King and the Kingdom of Heaven
The Body of Christ: A Reality
Let Us Pray
God's Plan and the Overcomers
The Glory of His Life
"Come, Lord Jesus"
Practical Issues of This Life
Gospel Dialogue
God's Work
Ye Search the Scriptures
The Prayer Ministry of the Church
Christ the Sum of All Spiritual Things
Spiritual Knowledge
The Latent Power of the Soul
Spiritual Authority
The Ministry of God's Word
Spiritual Reality or Obsession
The Spiritual Man

by Stephen Kaung

Discipled to Christ
The Splendor of His Ways
Seeing the Lord's End in Job
The Songs of Degrees
Meditations on Fifteen Psalms

ORDER FROM:

**Christian Fellowship Publishers, Inc.
11515 Allecingie Parkway
Richmond, Virginia 23235**